COOPERATIVE LEARNING IN THE CLASSROOM

Putting it into Practice

Wendy Jolliffe

Los Angeles • London • New Delhi • Singapore

First Published 2007. Reprinted 2008

SAGE Publications Ltd
1 Oliver's Yard
55 City Road
London EC1Y 1SP

SAGE Publications Inc
2455 Teller Road
Thousand Oaks
California 91320

SAGE Publications India Pvt. Ltd
B 1/I 1 Mohan Cooperative Industrial Area
Mathura Road, New Delhi 110 044
India

SAGE Publications Asia-Pacific Pte Ltd
33 Pekin Street #02-01
Far East Square
Singapore 048763

Library of Congress Control Number: 2006930287

A catalogue record for this book is available
from the British Library

ISBN 978-1-4129-2379-8 (hbk)
ISBN 978-1-4129-2380-4 (pbk)

Typeset by C&M Digitals (P) Ltd, Chennai, India
Printed in Great Britain by Cpod, Trowbridge, Wiltshire
Printed on paper from sustainable resources

CONTENTS

Wendy Jolliffe is a Lecturer in Primary at the University of Hull with a particular responsibility for literacy and early years. She was previously a Deputy Headteacher of a Primary School in Hull and a Curriculum Support Teacher for Literacy for Hull Children's Service. She has used cooperative learning extensively in teaching primary school pupils and students in Higher Education; in addition, she trains primary teachers in its methods. Her research interests focus on key factors in implementing cooperative learning. She is currently supporting a networked learning community of primary and secondary schools in developing cooperative learning.

Acknowledgements

I would like to thank the staff from the Bransholme Networked Learning Community schools and in particular the facilitators for their hard work and commitment to cooperative learning. I would also like to thank my husband, David, for his unfailing support.

HOW TO USE THIS BOOK

The format of this book consists of a range of activities to reinforce important aspects of cooperative learning. Key points will be summarised at the end of each chapter for ease and a separate section will outline staff development sessions. In addition, a school self-evaluation tool is set out in Chapter 5 to be completed at key points during implementation.

This book will provide the reader with a clear understanding of the following:

1. Learning for all: issues of inclusion and the impact of cooperative learning.

2. Providing for a range of learning styles and supporting personal, social and emotional development.

3. Strategies for effective talk in the classroom.

4. The impact of cooperative learning and issues in its use.

5. A phased implementation of cooperative learning.

INTRODUCTION

Cooperative Learning: What Is It and Why Does It Matter?

How this book supports learning and teaching in the classroom

This book not only ensures a clear understanding of cooperative learning and how it supports effective learning, but also provides step-by-step guidance on how to put it into practice in the classroom. It is designed to be used for whole-school professional development and each chapter sets out a range of activities for use in this way. Appendix 1 summarises this programme, giving timings for each session. The book can also be used by individual teachers or trainees who wish to find out more about cooperative learning and how to apply it in the classroom.

Understanding pedagogy

Pedagogy is a word that teachers tend to shy away from. Some notable academics, such as Robin Alexander,[1] have lamented a lack of clear pedagogy in the UK. Let us consider what the word itself means. The most common definition of pedagogy is: 'the science and art of teaching'. It involves the knowledge and skills that a teacher brings to bear to support the constant decisions that need to be made. It is not a static art or science: it should be dynamic and reflect ongoing technological and cultural changes. So what is an appropriate pedagogy for the twenty-first century? Robert Slavin, one of the originators of cooperative learning, exemplifies this point vividly when he describes the 'Rip Van Winkle effect' with respect to teaching:

> Imagine a doctor goes to sleep for 100 years and then wakes up. He decides to go to work and practise medicine. Imagine his surprise at the latest technology, methods and medicines, or indeed the reaction of other doctors or patients. Imagine instead a teacher who does the same and goes back to the classroom after 100 years. He goes to the front of the classroom and takes up his chalk, writes a few key points and then goes on to question pupils, to which individuals put up their hands to respond. Would anyone notice that 100 years have elapsed since he last taught?[2]

Figure I.1   Maslow's hierarchy of needs, reprinted with permission from John Wiley and Sons, Inc.

Food for thought indeed: has pedagogy not changed in 100 years? We have computers and interactive whiteboards and we are directed to teach 'interactively' by the Primary National Strategy. But what does that mean and how many teachers really understand it? Does holding up objects such as mini-whiteboards or number fans by pupils, consist of interactive teaching? Is it about open questioning? Research[3] has shown that most questions are closed and consist of the type of 'guess what is in my mind', that is, the teacher has a clear idea of the answer, and the children have to guess it. Have we really taken advantage of all we know about how we learn effectively, that learning does not take place in a vacuum? Crucial issues such as being in a physical state to learn, as we know from Maslow's hierarchy of needs (see Figure I.1), show that we need to feel secure, valued, and with our physical needs of food, heat, clothing, environment fulfilled. If we are in a state of distress, we know the brain reacts to protect us and the pathways to new learning are blocked. In Chapter 2 we examine this link to learning more closely, but meanwhile you may like to look at Appendix 2, which will help you review how well you fulfil pupils' needs. You can then discuss this with colleagues as a starting point to introducing cooperative learning.

As well as ensuring that pupils are able and ready to learn, the work of Vygotsky shows us that learning takes place with, and alongside, others. We need to orally rehearse what we are learning. We need to explain and elaborate not only to consolidate, but also by working alongside more proficient peers, we can take steps forward in our learning, or as Vygotsky described it, progress in our 'zone of proximal development'. William Glasser illustrates this by saying we learn:

10 per cent of what we read
20 per cent of what we hear
30 per cent of what we see
50 per cent of what we hear and see
70 per cent of what we discuss with others
80 per cent of what we experience personally
90 per cent of what we teach to others.

So, as this brief preamble shows, we know considerably more about learning than 100 years ago. But, returning to the example of Rip Van Winkle, how much have teachers put into practice? Over the past 30 years, key researchers such as Robert Slavin, Spencer Kagan, David and Roger Johnson, Shlomo Sharan, Richard Smuck, Elizabeth Cohen, Don Brown and Charlotte Thomson have been both researching and putting into practice a very different approach to the traditional method of IRF/E teaching (initiation–response–feedback/evaluation): that of cooperative learning. This book shows practitioners how to put theory into practice in their own setting. It also aims to put cooperative learning into the twenty-first century UK context using the author's experience of teaching cooperatively and supporting schools to implement it. Whilst the book is based on extensive research, it does not aim to analyse or synthesise this in depth. It aims to support teachers and schools to implement cooperative learning effectively.

What is cooperative learning?

It is important first to establish exactly what we mean by cooperative learning. We could say in essence *cooperative learning requires pupils to work together in small groups to support each other to improve their own learning and that of others.* However, it is not quite so simple, because there are variations on cooperative learning and some fierce arguments amongst academics as to the value of each, for example should it include any element of extrinsic reward or should reward be purely intrinsic? This book is not going to take a purist attitude, rather a pragmatic one. What is important is how teachers can plan for cooperative learning and manage it in the classroom, but fundamental to that is an in-depth understanding of what it is. Most researchers agree that to be truly cooperative, learning should consist of key elements and two of these are particularly vital:

1. **Positive interdependence –**' *We sink or swim together*'
   This requires each pupil in a small group to contribute to the learning of the group. Pupils are required to work in a way so that each group member needs the others to complete the task. It is a feeling of 'one for all and all for one'.
2. **Individual accountability –**' *No Hitchhiking!*'
   This means that each member of the group is accountable for completing his or her part of the work. It is important that no one can 'hitchhike' on the work of others. It requires each pupil in the group to develop a sense of personal responsibility to learn and to help the rest of the group to learn also.

Whilst researchers disagree about the other essential ingredients, many feel that one further aspect is necessary, what is called the 'lubricant of cooperative group work': interpersonal and small-group skills. These consist of two elements: the academic (task) skills, such as following instructions, staying on task, planning and reviewing progress, managing time, generating and elaborating on ideas. The second element concerns the interpersonal skills such as listening to

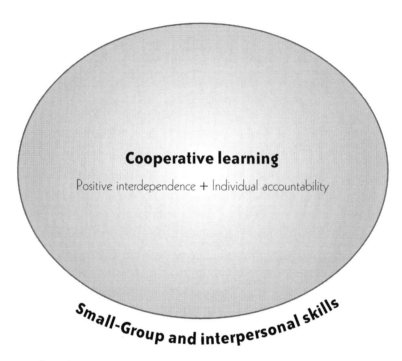

Figure I.2   Elements of cooperative learning

others, encouraging, achieving a consensus, conflict resolution, and valuing others. Figure I.2 shows these key elements visually.

Why is it different from group work?

As stated previously, cooperative learning has two main prerequisites. Tasks need to be structured to ensure pupils are interdependent and individually accountable; just putting pupils into groups does not mean they will work together cooperatively. Group work itself is nothing new or magical. Traditionally, primary schools have often organised pupils to sit in groups of four or six, although interaction between them may be very limited. The reason underlying this is the ethos of individual competition where pupils often complain: 'He's copying me!' In this situation where pupils are not required to work collaboratively to complete a task, they would often be better working alone. To become cooperative, groups must work together to accomplish shared goals. They need to discuss work with each other and help each other to understand it. Of course, this does not happen instantly, it is a gradual process aided by a clear teaching programme of small group and interpersonal skills together with tasks and teaching techniques that foster interdependence. A step-by-step programme will be provided in the following chapters to enable teachers to do this.

Teamwork – developing a necessary life skill

Many academics agree that humans have been successful as a species, not because we are physically strong, or able to camouflage ourselves, or run swiftly as some animals do, but because we are intelligent. But even this would not ensure our survival; what does is our ability to work with others to fulfil shared goals: to cooperate.

Teamwork is a well-known and sought after characteristic of professionals, and cooperation in many forms is a key aspect of modern life. It is therefore somewhat bizarre that schools are normally the least cooperative and, instead, the most competitive places. Most of the time, pupils work independently and compete with each other; hence the distress pupils feel if someone copies their work. It is not just pupils who work individually. Teachers, too, usually work individually in classrooms, lacking the support and help of colleagues. One of the major themes of this book is that cooperative learning necessitates a sea change in attitude from teachers and pupils, or put another way: *cooperative learning in the classroom requires cooperative learning in the staffroom.* It requires teamwork from teachers to support its use and teamwork from pupils to achieve its ends. A cooperative learning school becomes a community of learners with pupils and teachers alike working towards shared goals.

Learning to learn/creating a learning climate

To achieve such a community of learners it is necessary to create a learning climate, and this requires certain conditions to be met. At its heart is a supportive ethos that values and celebrates diversity. The use of language needs to be carefully examined to ensure it is of a 'no blame' nature and, most importantly, children's personal, social and emotional needs should be given priority. These are the necessary prerequisites for learning and the 'glue' for pupils working cooperatively.

The Primary National Strategy's professional development materials, *Excellence and Enjoyment: Learning and Teaching in the Primary Years,*[4] puts creating a learning culture and understanding how learning develops, as two central themes to effective learning. Indeed, it states its aim is for pupils, by the end of Key Stage 2, to be able to work well with others. It recognises that this requires a range of skills including:

Cognitive aspects of learning	Affective aspects of learning
• Enquiry	• Self-awareness
• Problem-solving	• Managing feelings
• Creative thinking	• Motivation
• Information processing	• Empathy
• Reasoning	• Social skills
• Evaluation	• Communication

The social and emotional skills, or affective aspects, have now been supported with a series of documents and professional development materials entitled *Excellence and Enjoyment: Social and Emotional Aspects of Learning* (SEAL),[5] to support teachers in providing a teaching programme for pupils. Research has also shown that programmes that teach social and emotional skills impact on pupils' academic skills, motivation, attendance and morale.

The professional development materials distributed by the Primary National Strategy provide a range of supportive documents and videos for schools to help develop a learning culture and, indeed, one of the sections deals with 'Classroom community, collaborative and personalised learning', including a short section on cooperative learning. However, this does not provide sufficient background or details of how to implement it. This book aims to do this and to show how it can be a vehicle for improving cognitive and affective aspects of learning.

Every Child Matters

The Children Act 2004 and *Every Child Matters: Change for Children* (2004) set out the framework for services for children to maximise opportunities and minimise risk. The main aspects of reform centre around five key themes: be healthy, stay safe, enjoy and achieve, make a positive contribution and achieve economic well-being. *Every Child Matters* makes important links not only between services for children but also shows that learning cannot occur unless all these needs are met. Working cooperatively with others can support these aims, as can be seen from its many proven advantages. As can be seen from Figure I.3, the outcomes and aims of *Every Child Matters* can be clearly mapped to the advantages of cooperative learning.

Advantages of working cooperatively

Cooperative learning is one of the most heavily researched areas of education. Studies[6] have shown three main categories of advantages: achievement, interpersonal relationships, and psychological health and social competence.

Improvements in learning have been shown through:

- greater productivity
- higher process gain (that is, more higher-level reasoning, more frequent generation of new ideas and solutions)
- greater transfer of learning from one situation to another
- more time on task
- greater problem-solving.

Improvements in interpersonal relationships have been shown through:

- promoting the development of caring and committed relationships
- establishing and maintaining friendships between peers
- a greater sense of belonging and mutual support
- improved morale.

Improvements in psychological health and social competence have included:

- higher self-esteem
- improved self-worth
- increased self-confidence
- greater independence
- supporting sharing of problems
- increased resilience and ability to cope with adversity and stress.

Cooperative learning
Advantages

Every Child Matters	Cooperative learning Advantages
Be healthy Physically healthy Mentally and emot[ional] Sexually healthy Healthy lifestyles Choose not to tak[e]	**Improved psychological health and social competence** Higher self-esteem Improved self-worth Promotes self-confidence Develops independence Supports sharing of problems Increased resilience and ability to cope with adversity and stress
Enjoy and achieve Ready for school Attend and enjoy s[chool] Achieve stretching national educational standards at primary school Achieve personal and social development and enjoy recreation [Stay safe] [su]pport the community Engage in law-abiding and positive behaviour in and out of school Develop positive relationships and choose not to bully and discriminate Develop self-confidence and successfully deal with significant life changes and challenges Develop enterprising behaviour	**Improved learning** Greater productivity Higher process gain (i.e. more higher-level reasoning, more frequent generation of new ideas and solutions) Greater transfer of learning from one situation to another More time on task Greater problem-solving
Achieve economic well-being Engage in further education, employment or training on leaving school Ready for employment Live in decent homes and sustainable communities Access to transport and material goods Live in households free from low income	**Improved interpersonal skills** Promotes the development of caring and committed relationships Helps establish and maintain friendships between peers A greater sense of belonging and mutual support Improved morale

Figure I.3   Mapping the aims and outcome of *Every Child Matters* with the advantages of cooperative learning

Now examine Figure I. 3 to see how the proven advantages of cooperative learning can support the aims and outcomes of *Every Child Matters*.

So why is it not widely used?

If cooperative learning has such an extensive pedigree, why are schools not using it more? This was a question that I puzzled over until, on further research and from use myself in the classroom, I realised it is crucial that pupils are given training and support in developing the interpersonal and small group skills necessary for effective cooperative learning. By just putting pupils together to work and providing some of the cooperative learning structures or techniques, will not guarantee success. A clear programme of teaching the skills required needs to be in place, which is valued and assessed in the same way as other areas of the curriculum. In Chapter 5 a staged approach to developing these skills is set out. Links are made to the Personal, Social and Health Education (PSHE) curriculum and the use of circle time, as well as the SEAL materials from the Primary National Strategy.

Another reason for a lack of either interest or success with cooperative learning is that it can be problematic. It requires pupils to talk, discuss and interact, which can, at least initially, make teachers feel a loss of control over a class. In addition, teachers have worried over the ability to effectively assess pupils as individuals when they work in a group. These issues are discussed at length and a range of solutions provided in Chapter 6. At the heart, perhaps, of any reluctance for teachers to use cooperative learning is what amounts to a totally different role for the teacher. The teacher becomes a facilitator of learning, organising, monitoring, supporting and intervening where appropriate. The teacher is not in the role of imparter of knowledge, firing questions at pupils – the 'chalk and talk' of common classroom practice. In effect, the teacher in cooperative learning has moved on a long way from the Rip Van Winkle example. He or she has become the teacher of the twenty-first century.

Points to remember

1. Learning is a social process which requires interaction amongst pupils.

2. Cooperative learning is not just group work – tasks are structured to necessitate the interaction of pupils in pairs/groups.

3. Advantages of cooperative learning include achievement, interpersonal relationships, psychological health and social competence.

4. Teachers need to understand the key elements and how to incorporate them successfully into lessons.

5. Cooperative learning is linked to social and emotional skills.

6. Cooperative learning can support the aims of *Every Child Matters*.

7. Pupils need support and training in interpersonal and small-group skills.

8. Cooperative learning in the classroom requires cooperative learning in the staffroom!

Further reading

Johnson, D.W., Johnson, R.T., and Holubec, E.J. (1994) *Cooperative Learning in the Classroom.* Alexandria, VA: ASCD.

Kagan, S. (1994) *Cooperative Learning.* San Juan Capistrano, CA: Kagan Cooperative Learning.

Slavin, R.E. (1995) *Cooperative Learning: Theory, Research and Practice* (2nd edn.). Boston, MA: Allyn & Bacon.

CHAPTER 1

Learning for All?

> This chapter helps analyse the essential ingredients for an inclusive classroom and provides support in auditing inclusive practice. It sets out the key principles of an inclusive curriculum and focuses on effective interactive methods of teaching. It shows, through examples, how cooperative learning is truly inclusive.

Inclusion is a key part of the education agenda. It is clearly related to basic human rights and the entitlement in schools derives from the United Nations Convention on the Rights of the Child (1989). Education can play a powerful role in ensuring that institutions adapt to meet individuals needs promoting *education for all*. Debates range from how we effectively meet all children's needs in mainstream schools, to accounting for a range of learning styles and ability. The issue of boys underperforming is also crucial and, as examination results are published, we see yearly the pattern of girls overtaking boys in a range of academic areas. Of course, these issues are complex and there is no easy solution, but ensuring maximum participation and engagement in the classroom is a start and, used effectively, cooperative learning can do just this.

Read the following 'Think about this' and reflect on the extent to which this is a common situation in classrooms.

Think about this 1.1

A typical classroom

A primary Year 6 class in an inner city school sit in rows facing the teacher. It is literacy and the teacher is delivering the whole-class, shared reading part of the lesson. The text is displayed on the interactive whiteboard and the teacher reads it in a variety of ways: with the class, to the class and selecting different pupils to read sections. A few children (usually the same ones) are eager to read, some are very engaged, and many are on automatic pilot: it is 11 a.m. and every morning at school they know the familiar routine. A few are disaffected and display attention-seeking behaviour, flicking rulers, drawing on mini-whiteboards. If one was to investigate further the challenging home circumstances that many had to deal with would reveal that being ready and able to learn was a real difficulty.

(Continued)

As the lesson progresses, the teacher tries to engage the class in discussion. Even though she endeavours to ask open-ended questions, a few children put up their hands eager to respond. An observer might notice the children who sit quietly and do not disturb the lesson, hardly saying a word. Do they learn from this type of whole-class teaching? Most teachers would say it is difficult to ascertain, except from the later work they produce. Some teacher will talk of reflecting on the school day and realising there are some children they have not spoken to at all.

In this and most classrooms, the ability differences are wide and children soon accept a pecking order and a self-concept of being clever or not. The concept of failure is soon learned and not so soon unlearned. Is the answer down to the ability of the individual teacher to engage all pupils?

Numerous studies have shown the drawbacks to this type of teaching,[1] particularly for low-achieving students.[2] So, how can the teacher be truly inclusive and ensure that all children are motivated and engaged in learning? To enable all children to make progress, schools are expected to implement the National Curriculum inclusion statement:

When planning, teachers should set high expectations and provide opportunities for all pupils to achieve, including boys and girls, pupils with special educational needs, pupils with disabilities, pupils from all social and cultural backgrounds, pupils from different ethnic groups including travellers, refugees and asylum seekers, and those from diverse linguistic backgrounds.[3]

This sets out three principles that are essential to developing a more inclusive curriculum:

1. Setting suitable learning challenges which relate to appropriate learning objectives by acceleration for some and tracking back for others.

2. Responding to pupils' diverse learning needs through a range of teaching styles such as more open-ended or extended tasks for the more able pupils, modelling and visual aids for English as an additional language (EAL) learners.

3. Overcoming potential barriers to learning and assessment for individuals and groups of pupils. This relates to the provision of access strategies such as providing alternatives to written recording or in maths the use of 100 squares or number lines.

The Primary National Strategy talks about 'interactive whole-class teaching'. This has not been well understood by teachers and one study[4] found 'interactive' consisted of superficial 'gimmicks' such as 'show me activities' and so on, rather than 'deep features' which encourage pupils to reflect on their thinking and support the joint construction of meaning. The use of extended questioning which supports higher-order thinking can be a powerful method of stimulating and evaluating pupils' thinking. One method which builds on this is 'dialogic teaching'[5] which consists of the following five elements:

1. It is collective – children work together on tasks, as a group or class.

2. It is reciprocal – teachers and children listen to each other and comment/share ideas.

3. It is supportive – children are supported to discuss their views freely.

4. It is cumulative – teachers and children build on each other's ideas to create coherent lines of thinking.

5. It is purposeful – teachers plan and steer classroom talk with specific purposes.

Dialogic teaching shares many of the purposes and methods of cooperative learning. In particular, strategic cooperative learning[6] brings together cooperative learning with cognitive and meta-cognitive strategies for learning. Here the use of a range of thinking skill approaches such as graphic organisers, and 'think aloud' strategies, together with the powerful combination of pupils working together cooperatively, makes for a very effective learning programme. This is explored further in Chapter 4.

The Primary National Strategy's approach has, more recently, through the professional development materials for *Excellence and Enjoyment*, attempted to clarify more discursive or interactive teaching, key elements of which are described as 'active listening' and 'involving children'. Strategies are offered for both, such as using visual aids and class discussion of what constitutes 'good listening' and a range of multi-sensory techniques by which to involve children. In addition, inclusion of all learners is recommended by techniques such as differentiated questioning, support and providing a range of tasks. All these go some way to supporting learning for all. However, teachers need support with the mechanism to carry it out. This mechanism needs to take the emphasis away from the teacher as the fountain of all knowledge and instead view the teacher as a co-learner or a co-constructor of knowledge with the pupils. The mechanism needs structures and tasks that can only be completed through valuing and supporting each other, working together through talk and active construction of meaning. It needs cooperative learning. As one research study amongst many shows, 'Cooperative learning has potential as a powerful teaching strategy in inclusive classrooms impacting both academic and social skills'.

Let us now look at a very different 'Think about this' to that of Think about this 1.1. Let us take the same class and subject and look at it cooperatively. Reflect as you read on the elements of inclusion: of ability, of gender and of background.

Think about this 1.2

A cooperative learning classroom

A primary Year 6 class in an inner-city school sit in groups of four or five facing each other. These groups are formed of mixed ability and gender and they have all spent some time over previous weeks creating a team identity by devising, amongst other things, team names and team raps. It is literacy and the teacher is delivering the whole-class, shared reading part of the lesson. She begins by introducing the lesson objective and then the focus for working cooperatively for the week (for example, 'helping and encouraging each other'). She then makes a link to the previous lesson and asks the children to think about what they remember.

(Continued)

After allowing time for this she asks them to share with their partner first, and then asks pairs to talk to the rest of their group. She checks that they are all ready to provide a response and each group has agreed on what key aspects of the previous lesson they learned. Then she asks one member of each group to report the findings of the group using a numbered heads strategy, which ensures that everyone is ready to answer. Different groups report back and then the teacher begins to look at today's text. Some children move their chairs to ensure they can see the text, and a passage is read together. At key points the teacher stops and asks questions to check understanding. Pupils are always given time to think and to talk about answers either in pairs or groups.

Those disaffected pupils with challenging home circumstances know that their teams need them, or they cannot succeed. In addition, they have had support in interpersonal skills or the affective elements of learning that would otherwise prevent them from being ready and able to learn. They feel wanted and included. Group members are often given roles such as the scribe, time manager, participation checker or materials organiser, and groups often soon identify team members' strengths and use them accordingly. Visual learners are often asked to draw the diagrams or mind maps, boys are often eager to physically re-enact scenes from a text read and those with good handwriting and spelling scribe the group's finished product.

Let us look at how cooperative learning is inclusive:

1. Questions are never asked of individuals. If a question is worth asking, it is worth asking of everyone.

2. Children work in heterogeneous groups, which consist of mixed gender, ability and background.

3. Children are supported and given training in interpersonal and small group skills. Regardless of background or home situation, there is no assumption that children can work with others effectively.

4. Every child contributes and their contribution is valued, indeed is crucial, to the success of the group.

5. Learning is active and social, not passive and as such it appeals to everyone, particularly boys.

6. It creates a mutually supportive classroom.

Gifted and talented pupils

A common criticism of cooperative learning has been that peer-mediated models of learning fail to consider the needs of the more able pupil who may require more independent learning and flexibility. However, a body of research has reported that gifted and talented pupils benefited just as much.[7] In fact, pupils gained in self-esteem and improved in academic skills, just as much in ability as in mixed ability groups.

As is discussed in later chapters, cooperative learning is a broad term and it incorporates different forms. Studies have shown that some cooperative learning methods may offer less challenge to gifted and talented pupils than to others; it is therefore important for teachers to understand the range of methods and the structure, and to select appropriately. For a summary of cooperative learning structures and the particular skills they support see Appendix 3.

Professional development activities

This chapter includes:

Activity 1.1: Reading and reflecting on two 'Think about this' scenarios – traditional whole-class teaching and whole-class teaching incorporating cooperative learning.
After reading each scenario, discuss the following questions:

1. How does each approach provide for children of different ability, including less able, gifted and talented pupils and EAL learners?

2. How does each approach provide for children with emotional and behaviour difficulties?

3. How does each approach provide for boys and girls and preferred learning styles?

4. How does each approach account for diverse social and cultural backgrounds?

Activity 1.2: Auditing inclusive practice.
This tool presents a starting point for schools to identify areas of strength and areas for development with regard to inclusion, or ensuring learning for all.

1. A typical three-part lesson	With difficulty	To a limited extent	Fairly well	Well (give examples)
Do you effectively involve all children in whole-class teaching and discussion?				
Do you use interactive strategies?				
Do you differentiate questioning?				
Do pupils generally listen attentively and show engagement?				
Does the level of whole-class work make it difficult for all children to access effectively?				
In guided or group work, do pupils genuinely work with others?				
Are pupils grouped by ability?				
Are all pupils able to access the work effectively?				
Are all pupils valued and their contributions welcomed?				
In plenary sessions, are all pupils able to contribute?				
How are EAL learners catered for?				
2. Playtimes and lunchtimes	With difficulty	To a limited extent	Fairly well	Well (give examples)
Is provision made for any children who are withdrawn or find it difficult to interact with others?				
Are there strategies for conflict resolution?				
Are there strategies for possible bullying?				
3. Whole-school activities	With difficulty	To a limited extent	Fairly well	Well (give examples)
Do children feel able to participate (e.g. in assemblies, sports days, celebrations, etc.)				
Are different social and cultural backgrounds catered for?				
4. Extra-curricular activities	With difficulty	To a limited extent	Fairly well	Well (give examples)
Can all children participate?				
Are specific needs catered for?				
Is the local community effectively involved?				

 Photocopiable: Cooperative Learning in the Classroom
Paul Chapman Publishing © 2007 Wendy Jolliffe

Points to remember

1. Traditional whole-class teaching fails to effectively promote inclusion or learning for all.

2. Interactive teaching that incorporates more than superficial 'gimmicks' can help engage pupils.

3. Cooperative learning, used effectively, engages all pupils in learning actively.

4. Cooperative learning strategies ensure interdependence of all members of a group.

5. Pupils need training in interpersonal and small-group skills; we are not born cooperative.

6. High- and low-ability students gain from working cooperatively.

7. Appropriately selecting activities and strategies supports effective cooperative learning.

Further reading

Hart, S., Dixon, A., Drummond, M.J. and McIntyre, D. (2004) *Learning without Limits.* Maidenhead: Open University Press

Sharan, S. (ed.) (1994) *Handbook of Cooperative Learning Methods.* Westport, CT: Greenwood Press

CHAPTER 2

Using Diversity as a Strength

This chapter explores celebrating diversity through multiple intelligences, and particularly examines the importance of developing emotional intelligence. How this is applied in the classroom and linked to cooperative learning is discussed.

One of the most effective ways of supporting inclusion in schools is by celebrating and valuing diversity. Howard Gardner's work on multiple intelligences[1] has revolutionised our thinking about ability, focusing instead on valuing different individual strengths. Instead of basing views on intelligence quotient (IQ) tests with an underpinning notion that intelligence is fixed, Gardner proposed that there was not one but many kinds of intelligences. Gardner originally identified seven main types of intelligence: verbal-linguistic, logical-mathematical, visual-spatial, bodily-kinaesthetic, musical-rhythmic, interpersonal and intrapersonal. He has since added to these and now includes naturalistic and existential, and indicates that there may be other categories. The key point to bear in mind is that this revolutionises the concept of IQ as an indicator of intelligence and instead acknowledges the many manifestations of ability.

Traditional schooling favours verbal-linguistic and logical-mathematical intelligences, which in turn disadvantages children who have strengths in other areas. However, in cooperative learning classrooms diversity is used as a strength, where each member of the group contributes in varied ways to a common goal.

Gardner's work is widely known and accepted in schools. But the interpretation can be problematic and Gardner has endeavoured to correct misinterpretations. We need to be mindful that his descriptions of intelligences are not fixed categories or pigeon holes into which we can put children; instead, they act as a guide to supporting and valuing children's many talents.

Schools are familiar with the notion of learning styles. The concept is derived from classification of psychological types, which shows that, as a result of heredity, upbringing and environment, individuals perceive and deal with information differently. Such classifications are also open to criticism; nevertheless, many schools have adopted a teaching approach known as 'VAK': visual, auditory and kinaesthetic. The underlying idea is that teachers should use a range of teaching styles to support children's preferred modes of learning. Visual learning can be supported by pictures, charts and diagrams, and so on. Auditory learning can take place through oral presentations and is often supported by learning mnemonics or singing rhymes. Kinaesthetic learning is supported by actions and practical tasks. There is a danger of regarding this too simplistically and thinking of individuals as having fixed learning styles. Most of us use a mixture of learning styles. In essence our learning experiences need to be varied to encourage children to use different learning styles strategically, to become efficient learners.

It is not just particular styles or strengths that we need to tap into in schools, but also dispositions to learning. Guy Claxton in his book, *Building Learning Power*,[2] cites the following powerful example, entitled 'learning the bagpipes in public':

> On his first morning as the new head of Staple Hill Primary School, he picked up his bagpipes and strode into assembly. Though they had been bought several weeks before, Pete had resisted the temptation to practise. He was a total bagpipe virgin, and he was going to attempt to play them for the very first time in front of several hundred unknown youngsters, not to mention the staff. Peter explained that he couldn't play the pipes, but he wanted to, and he was going to show them, week by week, his progress, and talk to them about his ups and downs. Then he put the bagpipes to his lips and blew. As expected, he made a truly dreadful noise, and after a shocked silence, the students burst into laughter.

Claxton goes on to show how the head used this as a powerful example to demonstrate the attitudes needed to succeed, what he calls the 4Rs: resilience (stickability), resourcefulness (being prepared to learn in different ways), reflectiveness (evaluating, planning and adapting) and reciprocity (interdependence, collaborating). This is about developing 'learning fitness' and can be likened to a sportsman or woman working on stamina, strength and coordination. So how do we do this mental workout? Claxton sees the first task as developing greater resilience and being able to 'lock onto learning and to resist distractions from outside and within'. Easier said than done, as many teachers would comment, faced by children who often are only too easily distracted.

Daniel Goleman's work on emotional intelligence[3] provides a fascinating insight into developing the ability to deny immediate self-gratification. Indeed, he states this ability is a greater predictor of later success for children than traditional IQ tests. He describes a study of 4-year-olds who were placed individually in a room with a researcher and in front of them were some sweets. They were told they could have two sweets if they could wait while the researcher went out of the room for a short time. The description of the children attempting to distract themselves from the lure of the sweets makes amusing reading. Some tried to cover their eyes, sing, talk to themselves, play games or even try to go to sleep. The study tracked down the children as they graduated from high school much later and found that those children who managed to resist temptation and not eat the sweets became better adjusted people, able to cope with setbacks and stress. The children who had grabbed the sweets had a more troubled psychological picture. They had become less confident socially, more indecisive and lacking in self-esteem.

So we need to delay self-gratification. Children need to learn that to delay getting an instant reward pays off. But how can we support this in school and develop good learning dispositions? Claxton suggests the following:

- ■ **Managing distractions:** some of these are easy to eliminate, such as basic needs – being tired, hungry or thirsty makes it hard to concentrate. But other things impact also, such as being uncomfortable or too much noise around. It is about being able to diminish distractions and often this is very different for each individual. Some can work with blaring music, others need silence. As teachers we often need to manage these for children. But how can we help them to develop the ability to block out what is around them? Often this is through interesting and stimulating tasks, pitched at the right level. Sometimes it is by modelling being absorbed, for example, in nowadays infrequent silent reading time. How often do teachers sit absorbed in a book at the same time as the children are reading? Children learn from such examples.

Some time ago a clerk in an office I was working in, recited to me her experience commuting to work on the train. She had witnessed something she found incredible. The person in front of her had sat down and opened her book. During the whole of the 50-minute journey, which was typically crammed with commuters, the person opposite had not looked up once. Her eyes had scanned the words and her hands had turned the pages, but she was totally absorbed in another world. It was what the psychologist Mihaly Csikszentmihalyi[4] calls 'flow' and the young clerk I worked with had, to my surprise, never experienced it.

Flow is the ability to get lost in learning; a state of being utterly lost in what you are doing and in this state, emotions are channelled and aligned with the task in hand. It is when you are stretched to your limits and feel spontaneous joy and intrinsic reward. Entering such a state is the ultimate in avoiding distractions. Once experienced and fostered, this can be a life-changing experience; one we need to promote in young children.

■ **Noticing and identifying significant detail** is a further skill that supports a resilient attitude to learning – a skill that can be improved with practice. This is often helped by being alongside others who are proficient and able to demonstrate and verbalise their skills. It is supported by the child taking on the role of apprentice with a more skilled peer or adult.

■ **Perseverance is another aspect of resilience:** developing the skill of keeping going when faced with difficulties, re-establishing lost concentration, not giving up and trying different routes. Children need to realise that learning is not easy: they may not understand something straight away and being bright does not mean that you always learn things easily. It means you persist. There are subtle messages here that children can easily pick up from teachers – messages we need to avoid conveying.

Now read Think about this 2.1 and discuss how you could support the child.

Think about this 2.1:

I can't do it!

Craig sits eagerly in an art lesson. There is a visitor today come to show the children how to draw buildings. The children watch carefully and then it is their turn to have a go. Craig picks up his sheet of paper and a pencil and begins to draw the outline of the building. The teacher circulates to help and encourage everyone. Suddenly there is a cry from Craig: 'Oh no!' But before anyone can do anything he erupts in a fury screwing his paper up in a ball and flinging it across the room. He sits slumped in despair. The visiting artist goes to speak to him. 'Whatever is the problem?' he asks. 'I can't do it. I can't draw. I will never be able to,' he responds. 'Of course, you can,' says the visitor. 'You are just learning and you have to practise. Let's look at how far you got.' A look at the screwed-up drawing reveals that the

(Continued)

picture was taking shape. But Craig points to a window that is not quite the right size or shape. 'Well, don't worry about that,' says the visitor 'Let me see how you can change it.' No matter how hard he tries, Craig won't listen; if he can't do it straight away he gives up. Bubbling over with self-doubt and lack of self-esteem he sinks into despair and refuses to take part in the rest of the lesson.

Craig is a not untypical child who has not developed good learning dispositions. At the heart of such dispositions is the ability to harness our emotions fruitfully, so they do not disrupt our more rational thoughts. We need to develop emotional intelligence. So, if we are going to help children like Craig we need to be clear what emotional intelligence consists of and how to support its development. Let us now look more closely at what this involves, at what Daniel Goleman calls 'emotional intelligence'.

What are the characteristics of emotional intelligence?

- To be able to get on well with others in a group.

- To be at ease with oneself through awareness of own abilities.

- To be assertive rather than aggressive.

- To be able to recognise and control emotions.

- To understand that emotions can impact on our behaviour and reflect on this.

- To have empathy for others.

Emotional intelligence can be summarised as consisting of five main domains:

1. **Knowing one's emotions.** This relates to self-awareness: recognising and monitoring feelings.

2. **Managing emotions.** Having recognised emotions, it is important to control or use them effectively, in order to avoid excessive anxiety or feelings or failure.

3. **Motivating oneself.** This concerns utilising emotions to support a goal and involves delaying gratification, being able to get into the 'flow' state to accomplish outstanding performance.

4. **Recognising emotions in others.** Building on self-awareness is awareness of others: empathy, a fundamental 'people skill'.

5. **Handling relationships.** This follows from being able to control one's own emotions, being able to work harmoniously with others and to develop a sense of belonging.

These aspects that make up 'emotional intelligence' underpin working with others. One of the key themes of *Every Child Matters* is to be healthy, both physically and mentally. Emotional intelligence plays a crucial role in being healthy and as the Department for Education and Skills

Domain	Behaviour	Teaching strategies
1. Self-awareness	• Identify, recognise and express feelings • Recognise that context affects the acceptability of different behaviours • Aware that our feelings affect our behaviours • Aware that our thoughts affect our feelings and behaviours	Team-building projects Social skills groups Circle time Challenging questions
2. Managing emotions	• Express emotions in helpful ways • Can calm down when necessary • Have strategies for coping with anger • Seek support when needed • Change feelings by reflection	Role play Circle time Teaching calming down strategies Support strategies: time out
3. Motivating oneself	• Set personal goals • Break down goals into small steps • Concentrate and resist distractions • Bounce back after disappointment • Delay gratification	Individual target setting Support different learning styles Celebrate achievements Cooperative groupwork
4. Recognising emotions in others (empathy)	• Recognise the feelings of others • Understand others' points of view • Value and respect the feelings and beliefs of others • Understand actions affect others	Role play Circle time Playground buddies Counselling skills Conflict resolution strategies Cooperative groupwork
5. Handling relationships (social skills)	• Belong to a community • Understand rights and responsibilities • Make and sustain friendships • Be assertive when appropriate • Work with others in a group	Conflict resolution strategies Role play Cooperative groupwork

Figure 2.1 The domains of emotional intelligence

(DfES) *Guidance on the 'Social and Emotional Aspects of Learning' (SEAL)* shows: 'The development of emotional and social competence and well-being can reduce mental health problems of young people and their teachers'.[5]

In addition, developing emotional intelligence is the cornerstone of cooperative learning. But, before we can look further at working cooperatively we must consider this in more detail. Examine the grid in Figure 2.1 and add any further activities you undertake in school.

Applying emotional intelligence in the classroom

Since the publication of Daniel Goleman's book on emotional intelligence, teachers have become increasingly fascinated by its implications. Some feel that he has overstated the case of its importance. Nevertheless, teachers generally recognise the impact of an inability to understand ourselves and others and control our emotions, on academic progress.

So how can teachers support emotional intelligence and can it be taught? My experience of teaching in a primary classroom is that it needs a specific programme, timetabled every week, given key importance and to be part of a whole school ethos. There is a range of published programmes (see websites at the end of the chapter) for schools to choose from as well the Primary National Strategy programme *Excellence and Enjoyment: Social and Emotional Aspects of Learning*, known as SEAL. This package supports professional development and provides a framework and a wide range of teaching materials from Foundation Stage to Year 6. It states: *'Social, emotional and behavioural skills underlie almost every aspect of school, home and community life, including effective learning and getting on with other people. They are fundamental to school improvement'.*[6]

Therefore emotional intelligence underpins the ability to work and get on with others. But if we are to support children in using their emotional intelligence to support their learning, they need to work together with others cooperatively. Figure 2.2 lists strategies that support emotional intelligence in the classroom. Review this list with colleagues to decide how to improve your provision.

In Chapter 5 we look closely at cooperative learning strategies to support emotional intelligence and the 'affective' domains of learning (shown by the five key aspects of emotional intelligence) linked to the cognitive domains of learning, described as consisting of reasoning, evaluation, creativity, enquiry, problem-solving and information processing. The research evidence is strong[7] into the impact of cooperative learning which shows how working cooperatively improves social skills and emotional intelligence.

Professional development activities

This chapter has included the following CPD activities:

Activity 2.1: Reading Think about this 2.1 followed by discussion of how you could support this child.

Activity 2.2: Domains of emotional intelligence. Reading and adding activities to the grid in Figure 2.1.

Activity 2.3: Strategies to support emotional intelligence. Reviewing and auditing provision in school in Figure 2.2.

Strategy	Focusing	Developing	Establishing	Enhancing
Procedures for establishing rights and responsibilities of pupils are set up (i.e. involvement in class and school rules).				
Pupils are involved in decision-making with class meetings and school council				
Circle time is used effectively, including establishing ground rules and following a planned structure.				
A programme for teaching the five key elements of emotional intelligence is in place and pupils understand success criteria and set goals accordingly.				
1. Self-awareness is taught through: providing opportunities for reflection through (AfL)* and setting goals, helped to identify and express a range of feelings.				
2. Managing feelings is taught through: a range of calming down strategies, understanding effects of emotions, being able to reflect on feelings and knowing where to go for support.				
3. Motivating ourselves is taught through: support in setting achievable goals, knowing how to break down goals into small steps, understanding the need to persist.				
4. Empathy is taught through: recognising the feelings of others, understanding others' points of view.				
5. Social skills is taught through: active listening, conflict resolution procedures, assertiveness training, communication skills.				

* = Assessment for Learning

Figure 2.2 Strategies to support emotional intelligence

Photocopiable: Cooperative Learning in the Classroom
Paul Chapman Publishing © 2007 Wendy Jolliffe

Points to remember

1. There are many types of intelligence, and different learning styles, but we should be wary of oversimplifying or putting children into neat pigeon holes.

2. We need to support children in developing learning habits or dispositions.

3. To cope successfully with life as well as academic learning, it is important to develop emotional intelligence.

4. Applying the skills of emotional intelligence in the classroom requires a whole-school, systematic teaching programme.

5. Utilising emotional intelligence – both intrapersonal and interpersonal skills – requires interaction with others.

6. Teaching cooperatively supports and develops emotional intelligence.

 Further reading

Claxton, G. (2002) *Building Learning Power*. Bristol: TLO Ltd.

DfES (2005) *Guidance on the 'Social and Emotional Aspects of Learning' (SEAL)*. (Ref: DfES 1319-2005.) London: DfES.

Goleman, D. (1995) *Emotional Intelligence*. New York: Bantam Books.

Goleman, D. (1998) *Working with Emotional Intelligence*. London: Bloomsbury.

Weare, K. (2004) *Developing the Emotional Intelligent School*. London: Paul Chapman Publishing.

 Websites and social and emotional learning programmes

Campaign for Learning, www.campaign-for-learning.org.uk

CASEL (The Collaborative for Academic, Social and Emotional Learning), www.casel.org

Emotional Literacy Education and Self-Knowledge, www.emotionalliteracyeducation.com

Excellence and Enjoyment: learning and teaching in the primary years (DfES 0518-2004 G) www.standards.dfes.gov

Excellence and Enjoyment: social and emotional aspects of learning (DfES 1378-2005 G) www.standards.dfes.gov.uk/banda

Jenny Mosley Consultancies/Positive Press Ltd, Whole School Quality Circle Time Model, www.circle-time.co.uk

Kids EQ: The Children's Emotional Literacy Project, www.kidseq.com

Lucky Duck Publishing, Sage Publications and Paul Chapman Publishing, www.luckyduck.co.uk

SAPERE (Society for the Advancement of Philosophical Enquiry and Reflection in Education), www.sapere.net

School of Emotional Literacy, www.schoolofemotional-literacy.com

SEAL – Society for Effective Affective Learning, www.seal.org.uk

The Incredible Years, www.incredibleyears.com

The National Emotional Literacy Interest Group, www.nelig.com

Transforming Conflict, www.transformingconflict.com

CHAPTER 3

Talk, Talk, Talk

This chapter looks at the role of talk to support learning. It provides strategies for effective talk in the classroom and provides practitioners with a communications skills programme. These are crucial to developing cooperative learning.

Learning requires interaction and not only does this need interpersonal skills, it also requires the skills of communication. Research shows a clear link between talk and learning.[1] It is surprising, therefore, that this is a factor that was not recognised until relatively recently. Spoken language was largely ignored as a key part of the school curriculum until the 1960s and it was not until the National Oracy Project, in the late 1980s and early 1990s that things began to really change. The following depicts what it is like to be a pupil in a traditional classroom:

Rules for being a good pupil:

- Listen to the teacher, often for long periods of time;

- When the teacher stops talking, bid properly for the right to speak;

- Answer questions to which the answer will be judged more or less relevant, useful and correct, by a teacher who is seeking not to know something, but to know if you know something;

- Put up with having anyone's answer treated as evidence of a common understanding or misunderstanding, so that the teacher will often explain something again when you understood it the first time or rush on when you are still struggling with what was said before;

- Look for clues to what a right answer might be from the way a teacher leads into a question, and evaluates the responses;

- Ask questions about the administration of the lesson but not usually about its content (and certainly never suggest that the teacher may be wrong);

- Accept that what you know about the topic of the lesson is unlikely to be asked for, or to be accepted as relevant, unless and until it fits into the teacher's frame of reference.[2]

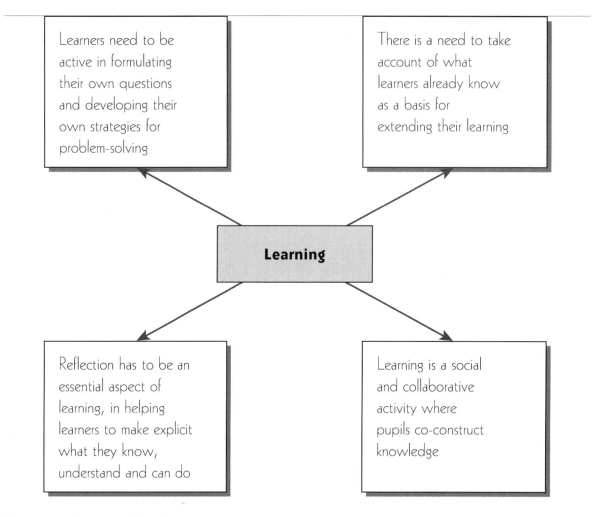

Figure 3.1 Aspects of learning

The fact that research that has shown that teachers' questions predominantly consist of closed questions supports the rather damning picture painted above. This was addressed by the work of the National Oracy Project which resulted in the centrality of talk to learning being developed by thousands of teachers in a variety of exploratory and innovative ways. As a direct consequence, in the 1989 National Curriculum, Speaking and Listening was included as a separate attainment target.

Activity

Working with colleagues, examine the ingredients for effective learning shown in Figure 3.1. Take each one in turn and discuss:

1. the extent that talk is required

2. the issues involved in putting the ingredients in place in the classroom.

Learning therefore involves the following aspects:

■   It is active.

■   It is social.

- It needs to link with existing knowledge.

- It needs to include reflection or 'meta-learning'.

The role of talk in learning was investigated by the Russian psychologist Lev Vygotsky[3] who looked at the link between language and thinking. He saw our use of language as serving two purposes, first as a 'cultural tool' for sharing and developing our knowledge to support our social life and second as a 'psychological tool' to help organise our individual thoughts. He also felt that these two aspects are integrated to help us become active members of communities. Most children have heard the phrase 'Sticks and stones may hurt our bones, but words will never hurt us', but how wrong this is when we think that as Neil Mercer describes: *'Wars have ended, careers have been ruined and hearts have been broken because of what was said or written'.*[4] It is therefore easy to see that language can be effectively channelled to provide a crucial tool for learning.

So if talk supports learning why has pedagogy not altered as a result? The following are some possible reasons:

- the individualistic and competitive ethos that has prevailed in schools

- an assumption that communication is entirely a matter of information transfer

- the practice that talk is strictly controlled and directed rather than a resource to be encouraged and exploited as a powerful means of learning

- the pervasive nature of oracy, that is, it happens anyway so why plan for it?

The National Literacy Strategy recognised the central part of speaking and listening in developing literacy, but excluded it from the Framework for Key Stages 1 and 2. In 1999, QCA produced a document, *Planning for Speaking and Listening in Key Stages 1 and 2,* which attempted to bridge the gap. In response to widespread criticism of the National Literacy Strategy, a revision of this QCA document was made in order to integrate speaking and listening into the National Literacy Strategy Framework for teaching[5]. This has also gained added emphasis with the Excellence and Enjoyment professional development materials. The revised Literacy Strategy Framework in 2006, however, will include speaking and listening more explicitly. Hopefully, speaking and listening will begin to achieve its rightful status of underpinning language and cognitive development.

Strategies for effective talk in the classroom

For effective talk to take place, children first need support in developing communication skills and, second, opportunities to practise them in a range of circumstances. Useful guidance is provided by Peter Kelly[6] such as developing ground rules for talk, as well as exploring active engagement, probing and question raising, and helping others through talk.

Children need to learn that communication is a two-way process and that the core ingredients are honest talk and active listening, and teachers need to act as models for both. Some of the key issues that underpin effective communication are:

- that non-verbal messages contribute

- that humans use words to stand for thoughts, feelings and actions, therefore words are symbols

- cultural differences – a need to be aware that some cultures view eye contact as disrespectful.

The following activity with children is one way of highlighting the importance of non-verbal communication.

The window dresser

Children work in pairs and imagine they are on different sides of a glass window. They take it in turns to pick up a card (see examples below) and have to give the message to their partner without speaking

Examples:

Will you come to for a bike ride with me?
Will you play football with me?
Get out quick – the building is on fire!
Help! I've cut myself!
Your flies are undone!

Active listening

Linked to verbal and non-verbal communication is the process of active listening. This is a vital feature of effective communication and needs to be explicitly taught. We often ask children to listen or to watch but what they actually do is see and hear. Thinking and reflection must be involved if children are to learn. The following needs to be made clear:

1. Use the term 'active'. Listening is not passive but something you need to be actively involved with.

2. Discuss body language, and expectations of what should be seen and heard in the classroom if children are listening.

3. Listening is an active process that has three basic steps:

   (a) Hearing: this means listening enough to catch what the speaker is saying. For example, say you were listening to a report on zebras, and the speaker mentioned that no two are alike. If you can repeat the fact, then you have heard what has been said.

	Teaching strategies	Notes
1. Establish the need for active listening	a) Role play in pairs to demonstrate effects of not listening (e.g. showing lack of eye contact, bored body language (yawning, etc.), fiddling with objects. Pupils take turns to act out each role (talker or listener). Pupils share how they felt as they were talking and their partner was not listening. b) Role play interruptive listening with pupils in same pairs All the As talk on a subject they choose for one minute while all the Bs interrupt and keep bringing the topic back to themselves. Swap on signal so that all the Bs talk about their subject while being interrupted. Pupils share their feelings this time.	
2. Defining the skill	Use a T chart (draw a large T on the board or large paper with either side of the T marked 'sounds like' and 'looks like' With the class draw up a list of what the skills should sound like and look like. A double T chart can be used which also includes 'feels like'. This can then form a poster in the classroom for constant reference while the skill is practised and refined.	
3. Guided practice	Roles-play active listening using the rules for listening on T chart. Provide opportunities for pupils to practise with corrective feedback. The teacher monitors, observes, intervenes, coaches, reinforces and encourages. Groups reflect on how well they practised the skill and how they could become more effective in using it.	
4. Generalised application of the skill	Once the skill has been established, the teacher provides opportunities for using the skill in a range of contexts. Focus on the skill can be for a specified period of time and pupils reminded along with the objective of the lesson that this skill will be assessed.	

Figure 3.2   Stages in teaching active listening

(b) Understanding: the next part of listening happens when you take what you have heard and understand it in your own way. Let us go back to that report on zebras. When you hear that no two are alike, think about what that might mean. You might think, 'Maybe this means that the pattern of stripes is different for each zebra.'

(c) Judging: after you are sure you understand what the speaker has said, think about whether it makes sense. Do you believe what you have heard? You might think, 'How could the stripes be different for every zebra? But then again, the finger-prints are different for every person. I think this seems believable.'

Activity

Review the stages in Figure 3.2 for teaching active listening, to add or amend them to fit with your current school practice.

Active listening is therefore a key element in effective communication. The following strategies also support communication skills.

Receiving and sending skills

Distinguishing between receiving skills and sending skills is a first step. Receiving skills are those that relate to our understanding of the message relayed. Sending skills relate to the ability to get a message across. The following activities can be useful in supporting the development of these skills.

■ Making it clear: provide pupils with a rather obscure statement (the statement itself depends on the age group), for example 'I need someone who would be willing to leave what they are doing and to collect something from class 4.' Ask pupils to work with a partner to then restate the message in a limited number of words clearly. They then have to ask their partner to restate the message.

■ Say what you did: here pupils in pairs are given a series of situations and statements of what action they took (pictures can also be used). They have to describe accurately what they did and try to get their partner to understand how they felt without describing it. Situations could include losing their pet, getting lost in the shopping centre, breaking a special toy, and so on. The partner then has to say how he or she felt.

■ How did you feel when … : here pupils work with a partner and in turn they think of a situation when they felt an extreme emotion, such as fear, sadness or happiness, and have to try and ensure their partner understands how they felt. Cards showing faces with different expressions could be provided and in turn they take a card (without showing their partner) and think of a time when they felt that way. They then talk about it. The partner then relays how they felt by saying 'When you … you felt very …'.

These strategies need to be developed into a coherent teaching programme as part of PSHE, ensuring that pupils develop the two-way skills of receiving and sending information. Appendix 4 provides guidance on developing such a programme.

Issue	Solution	Notes
Getting pupils' attention when the classroom is noisy	Zero noise signal (such as a raised hand)	
Noise levels when pupils are working in groups	Discussing and devising strategies with the class for '20 cm voices' Appointing noise monitors	
Dominance by some pupils	Careful pairing and grouping to ensure a mix of personality and gender-specific roles in groups	
Encouraging shy or unconfident pupils	Paired support Teacher modelling and support specific roles in groups	
Time to teach communication skills	Produce long- and medium-term plans showing specific teaching (in PSHE and literacy) and links with other subjects	

Figure 3.3   Managing talk in the classroom

Ⓟ Photocopiable: Cooperative Learning in the Classroom
Paul Chapman Publishing © 2007 Wendy Jolliffe

The role of the teacher

The following factors also contribute to the necessary classroom ethos for developing talk:

1. Receptiveness to pupils' ideas.

2. Equality, not just control or domination.

3. Openness and honesty.

4. Warmth and friendliness: smiling, eye contact, reassuring gestures, not on a 'stage' but walking around the classroom.

5. Respect for pupils' feelings (empathy) putting themselves in pupils' shoes.

6. Sensitivity to outcasts – observing possible signs and making efforts to help.

7. Sense of humour – jokes and laughing at themselves, but not other pupils.

8. Caring attitude – show that they care more for pupils than anything else.

The use of circle time, adhered to correctly, also provides a vital strategy in supporting communication skills (see Chapter 2). For other ideas, see also *Speaking, Listening, Learning: Working with Children in Key Stages 1 and 2* and *Speaking, Listening, Learning: Working with Children Who Have Special Educational Needs.*[7]

Managing talk in the classroom

We have looked at the need for talk in the classroom for learning and also how to teach communication skills. Many teachers will say that talking is not the problem it is more a matter of 'how to shut them up!'

Activity

Now look at Figure 3.3 Review the possible issues and suggested solutions, adding and amending where appropriate.

Cooperative learning as a vehicle for effective talk

If the overriding premise is that talk is a necessary feature of learning, then obviously it is important to ensure that such talk is productive and not off task. Providing cooperative learning opportunities for pupils in pairs and small groups can ensure that pupils talk meaningfully and in relation to the task. They have to talk to succeed in the task and they are motivated to succeed through the task being interdependent, that is 'we sink or swim together'. In the next two chapters we look in more detail at what cooperative learning involves and how to implement it effectively.

Professional development activities

This chapter has included the following continuing professional development (CPD) activities:

Activity 3.1: The ingredients for effective learning. Discussing:

1   the extent that talk is required

2   issues involved in putting the ingredients in place in the classroom.

Activity 3.2: Active listening. Reviewing the stages for teaching active listening, in the light of current school practice.

Activity 3.3: Managing talk in the classroom. Possible issues and solutions.

Points to remember

1.   Talk is a crucial factor in effective learning, but only since the National Oracy Project has it been viewed as such.

2.   Effective talk requires communication skills, which need a clear teaching programme.

3.   Active listening is fundamental to good communication.

4.   Talk requires careful classroom management strategies.

5.   The role of the teacher in providing the right classroom environment for talk, as well as teaching the skills and modelling good practice, is the key.

6.   Talk requires carefully structured interaction: it requires cooperative learning.

Further reading

Corden, R. (2000) *Literacy and Learning through Talk: Strategies for the Primary Classroom.* Buckingham: Open University Press.

Smuck, R.A. and Smuck, P.A. (2001) *Group Processes in the Classroom.* (8th edn). New York: McGraw-Hill.

CHAPTER 4

Cooperative Learning and How It Can Help

This chapter explores cooperative learning in depth through examining its key elements. It presents a brief summary of research into the benefits of cooperative learning. Different approaches and how to provide the right environment for cooperative learning to flourish are discussed.

What is cooperative learning?

As stated in the Introduction, cooperative learning requires pupils to work together in small groups to support each other to improve their own learning and those of others. To work effectively certain key elements need to be in place. The following five elements are essential and these are known by the acronym 'PIGS F':

> **P**ositive interdependence
>
> **I**ndividual accountability
>
> **G**roup processing
>
> **S**mall-Group and interpersonal Skills
>
> **F**ace-to-face interaction.

Read through the description of these key elements, shown on Figure 4.1, and then, working with colleagues, construct a graphical representation of these, using a diagram, cartoon and/or key words to show what is distinctive about each element.

Supporting the key elements of cooperative learning

The following sub-sections describe methods that can ensure the key elements are in place.

1. Ensuring positive interdependence

Without the above five key elements of cooperative learning, it will not take place effectively. However, one of these elements is more crucial than the others in order to ensure its success:

1. Positive interdependence

Pupils must feel that they need each other and, in order to complete the group's task, that they 'sink or swim' together. They need to feel that they cannot succeed unless everyone does in the group. Some ways to create this feeling are through establishing mutual goals (students must learn the material and make certain group members also learn the material); joint rewards (if all group members achieve above a certain percentage on the test, each will receive bonus points); shared materials and information (one paper for each group, or each member receives only part of the information needed to do the assignment); and assigned roles (summariser, encourager of participation, elaborator, etc.).

2. Individual accountability

Cooperative learning groups are not successful until *every* member has learned the material or has helped with, and understood, the assignment. It exists when the performance of each individual pupil is assessed and the results are given back to the group and the individual. Thus it is important frequently to stress and assess individual learning so that group members can appropriately support and help each other. Some ways of structuring individual accountability are by giving each group member an individual test with feedback or by randomly selecting one member to give an answer for the entire group.

3. Group processing

Processing means giving pupils time and procedures to analyse how well their groups are functioning and using the necessary skills. This reflection identifies group strengths and goals. It helps all group members achieve while maintaining effective working relationships among members. Feedback from the teacher and/or student observers on how well they observed the groups working may help processing effectiveness.

4. Small-group and interpersonal skills

Pupils do not come to school with the social skills they need to collaborate effectively with others, so teachers need to teach the appropriate communication, leadership, trust-building, decision-making and conflict-management skills to students and provide the motivation to use these skills in order for groups to function effectively.

5. Face-to-face interaction

There are two aspects to this. The first is the physical proximity needed for effective communication, or 'eye-to-eye and knee-to-knee'. The second is that it supports thinking skills by more active involvement with the task and greater discussion. Oral summarising, giving and receiving explanations, and elaborating (relating what is being learned to previous learning) are important types of verbal interchanges.

Figure 4.1   Key elements of cooperative learning (PIGS F)

1. Give each group a measurable task, which they clearly understand.

2. Structure goal interdependence so that group members believe they can only achieve success if the entire group does, for example, through providing tasks that can only be completed jointly.

3. Give each member of the group only a portion of the information, materials or other necessary items so that group members have to combine their resources to achieve their goals (known as resource interdependence).

4. Provide group rewards and celebrate their joint success. This can be helped by providing a group score when pupils are tested individually and putting this against a specified criterion.

Figure 4.2   Steps to achieving positive interdependence

positive interdependence, or as Alexander Dumas famously described the motto of the 'Three Musketeers', 'All for one and one for all.'

Look now at the steps to achieving interdependence (Figure 4.2).

Other types of interdependence which can support the key aim of mutual support are:

- role interdependence – assigning group, interconnected roles (such as reader, recorder, checker, equal participation monitor, and so on)

- identity interdependence – each group develops its own identity through names, banners, mottos, collages, raps, and so on

- fantasy interdependence – by placing pupils in hypothetical situations, such as survival on a desert island and achieving a consensus by selecting key items from a list.

2. Ensuring individual accountability

The aim of cooperative learning is not just to teach pupils to work together in a group, but also to give pupils the skills to work independently. In other words, what they can do with the help of others today, they may learn to do on their own tomorrow.

Individual accountability means that each member of the group must learn to be responsible for his or her own contribution, otherwise the success of the group will be in danger. Figure 4.3 provides key ways to encourage this.

3. Ensuring group processing

Groups need to learn to analyse their own progress and their ability to function as a group together. This is a clear developmental process and can enable control over the quality of the work produced. The Figure 4.4 can support this.

4. Supporting small-group and interpersonal skills

Developing these skills will require an ongoing programme to teach and practise them. The best way to achieve this is to follow the steps outlined in Figure 4.5.

1. Provide a safe environment where pupils feel able to respond in groups or with the whole class, without fear of ridicule, i.e. 'No put downs!' This is the fundamental ethos of the classroom necessary for cooperative learning to take place.

2. Random reporting to the class of the group's contribution, through the use of a structure such as 'numbered heads'. Here members of a group are given a number and then the teacher calls out a number when groups are ready to report, and that person has to speak for the group. Groups are not aware of which number will be called and therefore have to be sure that everyone is ready to respond.

3. Ask group members to explain their group's work to a member of another group.

4. Ask pupils to sign their work and include a code for 'completed' or 'best work' to foster a sense of pride in their own achievements.

5. Use of group marks where the individual scores are aggregated and these group marks are made public. This can instil a sense of personal responsibility to do well to support the group score.

Figure 4.3 Key ways to ensure individual accountability

1. Have a particular teamwork skill (such as everyone participating) as the skill of the week and remind groups of this at the start of a lesson. During the lesson provide constant praise and reinforcement to encourage the development of the skill. At the end of the lesson ask groups to evaluate their progress with the specified skill.

2. Ask pupils to set goals for themselves and their teams.

3. Ensure that time is provided for reflection, not just at the end of the lesson but at other key points.

4. When appropriate, ask groups to produce short evaluations of their work.

Figure 4.4 Making processing/reflection happen

1. Allocate a notice board in the classroom entitled: 'Skill of the Week'.

2. Select a skill (see page 69).

3. Introduce the skill.

4. Explain the role of the week, e.g. if it is 'staying on task' then the role might be 'Taskmaster' (for more information on roles, see pages 50–1 and Appendix 5).

5. Choose structures that support the specific skill (see Appendix 3).

6. Model the skill to the whole class and, where needed, to a group. Reinforce the skill by monitoring and rewarding groups.

7. Reflect on the skill through providing time for groups to discuss and, where appropriate, complete reflection forms.

Figure 4.5 Small-group skills programme

Small-group skills have a considerable amount of overlap with the communication skills discussed in Chapter 3, but it is important to bear in mind that particular skills support group work. Step 4 of implementing cooperative learning, in Chapter 5, explores this aspect in depth.

1. Ensure that for cooperative learning activities pupils are seated in small groups (preferably of four or a maximum of five) facing each other. This will usually consist of two tables with four chairs placed in pairs opposite each other.

2. Strengthen the interaction and discussion that underpins the thinking process. Structures that help include (see Appendix 3 for details):

    Summarising or paraphrasing what a partner has said using the paraphrase game

    Think/pair/square

    The grid

    Graphic organisers.

Figure 4.6   Checklist for face-to-face interaction

5. Ensuring face-to-face interaction

This element of cooperative learning consists of two aspects, the physical layout of the classroom and the interaction that occurs as a result. Look at the checklist in Figure 4.6 for achieving face-to-face interaction:

Types of cooperative learning

Cooperative learning utilises three types of cooperative learning groups.

1. **Formal cooperative learning groups:** these last from one lesson to a few weeks and need to consist of the following to work effectively:

    (a)   team-building activities to establish team identify and cohesion
    (b)   specific teamwork skills highlighted each lesson and/or week
    (c)   teacher monitoring and support for task and teamwork skills
    (d)   evaluation of learning and teamwork by pupils and teacher.

2. **Informal cooperative learning groups:** these last from a few minutes to a whole lesson and usually consist of 'turn to your partner' discussion or think/pair/share and can be extended from pairs to fours or eights (often termed 'snowballing').

3. **Cooperative base groups:** these usually last for a term or a school year and consist of heterogeneous cooperative learning groups with stable membership to build on support and encouragement to each other. The elements described in formal cooperative learning groups above will need to be incorporated and built on.

Using informal cooperative learning

Informal cooperative learning can be included in any lesson and principally involves the 'turn to your partner' type of activities. Structures that support this are:

Think-pair-share

- The teacher asks a question and then provides 'think' time.

- Pupils talk to a partner.

- Pupils share their answers.

Think-write-pair-compare

- Pupils jot down their thoughts.
- Pupils compare with a partner, which helps organise thoughts and ensures individual accountability.

Write-pair-switch

- Each pupil works alone to write a response to a question or prompt.
- Pupils pair and discuss their responses.
- Pupils switch partners and form a new pair. They tell their new partner about their former partner's response.

Pairs check/check and coach

- After working on a topic, teams (or the teacher) prepare a list of questions to check understanding.
- Pairs take it in turns to answer the questions, with the other partner prompting and coaching.

Flashcard game

- To support memorisation of facts (such as multiplication tables), pupils work in pairs with flashcards, showing question on one side, and the answer on the other.
- Pupils take turns to hold up questions and test each other on correct answers.

Timed talking

- Pairs are given roles of A and B.
- Partner A talks for 60 seconds.
- Partner B talks for 45 seconds.
- Partner A continues/summarises.

Now consider the structure of a typical three-part lesson (Figure 4.7), select a curriculum area and, working with a colleague, plan to include some of the paired activities above.

Understanding why cooperative learning works

Using cooperative learning structures both informally and formally can transform lessons into fun, interactive sessions where children are really involved in their learning. The two main reasons why this works are, first, motivational and, secondly, cognitive. Cooperative learning structures create a situation in which the only way group members can complete the task is if the whole group does. Therefore each member of the group must help others to do whatever is necessary to succeed and in a team this means that everyone needs to put in maximum effort or they will let their team down. In other words, *children are motivated to learn and work hard to support their team.* This is a transformation from the situation of the child who tries hard and in a traditional competitive classroom is identified as a 'teacher's pet'. In cooperative learning classrooms, children who try hard are helping each other and thus peer norms of maximum effort are produced. There is a range of research[1] to show that pupils' support for academic goals was an important predictor for their academic success.

Typical Lesson Structure		Year Group:	
Objective:		Cooperative learning skill(s):	
Success criteria:			
Introduction			Cooperative learning paired activities
Whole-class work			
Group/independent work			
Plenary			

Figure 4.7   Typical lesson structure

The second reason is cognitive, largely based on the social constructivist theory.[2] According to this, pupils working together cooperatively promote intellectual growth because they are able to support each other's next step in their learning. Their potential for learning is enhanced through working with a peer. In addition, cognitive elaboration theories state that, if information is to be retained, some kind of cognitive restructuring (putting information into a different format or words) needs to take place. One of the most effective means of doing this is to explain material to someone else; precisely what cooperative learning facilitates.

Summary of research findings

What are the key findings from research? Cooperative learning has been extensively researched. Syntheses of research have been carried out[3] which have shown three main categories of advantages of cooperative learning:

1. **Achievement.** Over 375 studies in the past 100 years have shown how working together to achieve a common goal produces higher achievement and greater productivity than working alone. Cooperative learning also results in process gain (that is, more higher-level reasoning), greater transfer of what is learned within one situation to another and more time on task.

2. **Interpersonal relationships**. Over 180 studies have been conducted since the 1940s, which have shown that cooperative learning experiences promote greater interpersonal skills.

3. **Psychological health and social competence.** Working co-operatively with peers and valuing co-operation, results in greater psychological health, higher self-esteem and greater social competencies than competing with peers or working independently.

Research in the UK

One recent major research project, completed in 2005,[4] aimed to address the gap between the potential of group work to influence learning, motivation and relationships, and the limited use of group work in schools in the UK. This project involved a framework with four key dimensions:

1. The classroom context: preparing the classroom and the groups.

2. Interactions between children: preparing and developing pupil skills.

3. The teacher's role: preparing adults for working with groups.

4. Tasks: preparing the lessons and group work activities.

Results from this large-scale project over four years have showed overall positive effects on pupils' academic progress.

The author's own research, working with a networked learning community in a social and economically deprived area in Hull, showed that cooperative learning is becoming embedded. This research highlighted the importance of a dedicated member of staff (a facilitator) to support and monitor the school's evolution of cooperative learning, together with strong networked support amongst schools. Schools have also received training on coaching and made links to this. Facilitators have met regularly with staff from the university to review progress, update their skills and produce supporting materials for the schools. This model of cooperative learning is developed using the five principles known by the acronym 'PIGS F' (see page 39) and the structures (shown in Appendix 3).

Paired work has become well established and most schools are making good progress in establishing group work.

Different approaches to cooperative learning

There are a range of approaches to cooperative learning, as outlined below; however, the step-by-step approach in this book consists of largely a mixture of David and Roger Johnson's approach and Spencer Kagan's structures. Elements from other approaches are included also, based on extensive use in the classroom of what is effective. Figure 4.8 itemises the range of approaches; for further information on each, see Further reading at the end of the chapter.

Cooperative learning and thinking skills

Incorporating Bloom's taxonomy of thinking[5] with cooperative learning can be a useful strategy to support higher-order thinking. According to Bloom's taxonomy, there are higher and lower levels of thinking. Working cooperatively can support the development of higher-order thinking such as analysis, synthesis and evaluation. Figure 4.9 is an example of a series of lessons applying cognitive and cooperative learning strategies to teaching writing.

Role of the teacher

The teacher's role in cooperative learning is fundamentally different from that in a more traditional model. It is vital that the teacher first provides the supportive classroom ethos to encourage cooperative learning and opportunities for team-building. Alongside this is the necessity for developing interpersonal skills as part of a planned programme. The teacher is often described as being 'a guide on the side, not a sage on the stage'[6] who undertakes the following:

1. Plans lessons that decide on (a) objectives, (b) size of groups, (c) how to group pupils, (d) group roles, (e) organisation of the classroom, and (f) materials needed.

2. Explains the task and the cooperative skill with criteria for the success of both.

3. Monitors and intervenes with groups where necessary.

4. Evaluates the quality and quantity of achievement and ensures that groups reflect on their achievement and effectiveness as a group and set goals for improvement. Celebrates achievement.

Type of cooperative learning	Brief outline
Complex learning, Elizabeth Cohen	This ensures that tasks incorporate various multiple intelligence factors so that all members of the class may have an opportunity to contribute.
Student teams (STAD), Robert Slavin	Teams usually consist of four members who are mixed in gender, ability and ethnicity. The teacher presents the lesson, and then pupils work in teams to ensure that all members have mastered the objective. Pupils then take individual tests on the material, and scores are averaged for teams and compared with past scores, with teams rewarded for meeting certain criteria.
Group investigation, Yael and Shlomo Sharan	A problem-solving approach which has four elements: investigation, interaction, interpretation and intrinsic motivation. It encourages higher-order thinking skills by comparing, contrasting and integrating a range of ideas, concepts and findings.
Jigsaw, Elliott Aronson	Each member of a group learns an essential part of a whole of a topic by working with a focus group and then helps the home group to combine the knowledge to complete the task.
The structural approach, Spencer Kagan	This incorporates setting up teams and then using structures or social interaction sequences, which enable the teacher to transform existing lessons into a cooperative format by using simple strategies. These strategies, or structures, are content-free mechanisms and widely transferable across the curriculum.
Learning together, David Johnson and Roger Johnson	This incorporates three types of cooperative learning (formal, informal and cooperative base groups) which should be integrated. Each cooperative lesson or activity should include the five essential elements (PIGS F). Lessons and classroom routines should be cooperative and make use of cooperative learning structures. The whole school should be organised in a cooperative team-based way. This results in the routine use of cooperative learning with teachers supporting each other in resolving issues and developing its use.
Strategic co-operative learning, Dan Brown and Charlotte Thomson	This combines cooperative learning and cognitive/meta-cognitive strategies for learning. Through use of multiple cognitive organisations of data, e.g. graphic organisers, cooperative learning becomes the platform for higher-order thinking.

Figure 4.8   Approaches to cooperative learning

Stage	Teaching emphasis	Application to teaching writing	Cooperative learning activities
Orientating	Orientating pupils to ways of processing information. Teaching content strategically so that pupils will begin to apply key information processes strategies.	Introduce use of graphic organisers linked to previous work. Pupils learn the general structure and how to make their own graphic organisers (e.g. writing frames).	Think-pair-share: to summarise key information and prioritise. Modified 'Jigsaw': pupils given partially completed graphic organisers, they then find information to complete it and teach others in their teams their findings.
Framing	Framing pupils' background knowledge-processing into a cognitive strategy.	Describing the writing strategy steps, discuss rationale for its use and application. Model the strategy steps using think-aloud techniques.	Think-pair-share: identify how this writing method links to their previous work on graphic organisers. Modified group investigation: discuss and identify how the steps are similar and different from what they usually do in writing.
Applying	Applying the strategy to meet the particular task. Integrating with ongoing instruction. Able to use independently.	Collaborate with pupils in writing tasks, integrating graphic organisers.	Team writing about content taught: teams use completed organisers to write about content provided by teacher. Group investigation with writing task: teams investigate information related to topic, create graphic organisers to share findings with class and plan and write report.
Extending	Use what was learned as a basis for understanding in different contexts.	Extending writing strategy to use in different genres and with a range of information.	Group investigation. Research and evaluation: teams engage in writing projects using the same strategy. They share and refine results.
Reflecting	Review strengths and weaknesses. Set goals for further development.	Review and formulate writing targets.	Paired tutoring and support. Group reflection, e.g. 'three stars and a wish'.

Figure 4.9   Lessons applying cognitive and cooperative learning strategies to teaching writing

Forming groups

The formation of groups is a key part of the teacher's role. There are three major ways to form groups in the classroom:

1. **Random selection**. This is useful at the beginning of a school year to help pupils to get to know each other. This can be done by numbering everyone in the class (1–4) and then asking all the 1s to form a group, 2s a group, and so on. With an uneven number, explain that any pupils left can be 'stars' for the day and can choose which group to work with. Ensure that each group comprises a maximum of five pupils.

2. **Pupil selection**. This can cause difficulties, reinforce social cliques in the class and result in 'off-task' behaviour if pupils choose according to friendship. If, on occasions, pupil selection is seen as desirable, it may be better for them to select by other criteria than friends, for example they write a favourite pop group, television programme or sport on a slip of paper and then form a group with others that like the same.

3. **Teacher selection**. This is generally the best way of forming groups to ensure the greatest effectiveness of cooperative learning. The aim is to mix abilities, genders and skills, that is, achieve heterogeneous groupings. (See the discussion in Chapter 1, particularly regarding 'gifted and talented pupils', for a rationale.)

Size of groups

As previously stated, groups should be kept small and the rule of thumb is 'four and no more'. When class numbers do not equally divide into fours, it is perfectly alright to have threes, or sometimes fives. The problems come when groups get to six as here groups tend to subdivide into two and lose cohesion. A sensible starting point is to have pupils work in pairs and then join with another pair, at first for a short time and as they develop the necessary skills, to do so for longer. The duration of groups can also vary, but researchers have found five to six weeks as ideal.

Roles in groups

When children first begin to work together in pairs or groups they may be unsure about what they have to do. Giving them a specific function or role within the group or pair will help them to take on responsibility for their own actions. The assignment of roles can help to:

- foster positive interdependence – everyone must play their part if the group is to succeed

- help develop teamwork – teachers can introduce skills and functions needed in a group through the use of assigned roles for specific tasks

- assigning roles moves responsibility into the group and away from the teacher.

There are many roles that can be assigned to children depending on the task to be undertaken. At its simplest, being a 'gofer' (resources manager), a scribe or a reporter, for a pair or a group, might be the starting point, as it devolves responsibility at a simple level. See Appendix 5 for a full list of roles.

The type of role a teacher chooses to assign will be dependent upon the age, the skill level of the children and the task to be undertaken.

Roles can be introduced one at a time so that children can become accustomed to they way they operate and the teacher can judge the effectiveness of each role. Children can be observed and chosen to act as good role models. The first roles will be 'maintenance' roles, designed to facilitate the smooth functioning of the group.

Roles should be taught in the same way as other cooperative skills. Explicit modelling by the teacher and constructing joint definitions with the class would be very beneficial. The use of role cards can be given to identify the children and act as cue cards. The allocation of roles can be teacher directed or at random, depending once again on how accustomed children are to working in this way.

Providing the right environment

One key aspect for pupils to work together cooperatively is to consider the actual physical set-up of the classroom. The reasons for this are as follows:

1. The physical arrangement gives clear messages about the teacher's values and expectations for behaviour. Desks in rows give a different message from desks in small groups or in a horseshoe arrangement.

2. Classroom design has been shown by research to affect pupil achievement, time on task and acoustics.

3. The layout impacts on opportunities for interaction, for example, as I commented recently to a group of trainee teachers in a formal lecture room, 'this is the worst kind of learning environment'. The lecture-room arrangement encourages students to sit passively listening to the lecturer, not engage in meaningful interaction with peers to support their learning.

4. Well-designed classrooms define learning patterns and support transitions from one type of activity to another (such as whole-class work with pupils seated in front of the teacher in a large space, and groups of tables and chairs for group and independent work).

Cooperative learning group work is generally best arranged with pupils working at tables that seat four, with pairs side by side. However, teachers may decide initially that pupils are not ready for this and do not have the social skills to be able to deal with this arrangement effectively. One solution is called 'huddles', which involves moving desks or pupils together only during cooperative work sessions. Enlisting the help of pupils to do this in a structured, careful way can be useful and, once they are accustomed to the procedure, it can be done quickly.

Managing cooperative learning

If cooperative learning is to work effectively, the teacher needs to develop some management techniques, because cooperative learning classrooms can be noisy places! The following management signals, once taught to a class, can be extremely effective and promote a positive atmosphere, not requiring the teacher to raise his or her voice to gain control.

1. The quiet signal

It is important to establish a signal that you use and pupils copy to indicate zero noise. One of the most common originates from the Cubs which is a raised hand. Here the teacher raises a hand and says nothing. He or she waits and as children notice the raised hand, they copy it, thus other children follow suit as they notice the raised hands. The teacher waits for everyone to be ready before speaking. Praise for those complying quickly, can reinforce the signal.

2. Reducing the noise level

When groups are working, noise level can become unacceptable. This can be helped by:

- having a signal to lower the volume, such as the palm of the hand horizontal and lowered slowly

- traffic light cards to show level of noise acceptable, which are placed on group tables by the teacher when monitoring the class – green for fine, yellow for need to lower the noise, red for being silent, counting to 10 before continuing

- assigning a noise monitor to the group

- using a random timer for pupils to stop and discuss in groups the noise level.

3. Movement around the classroom

Having a system for pupils moving to groups, clearing up at the end of a lesson, or any other transition can help, for example, 1-2-3 move:

- On the command of '1' (this can be silent with just 1 finger raised) pupils stand behind their chairs (or close their books, and so on).

- On the command of '2' pupils face the direction they are moving in.

- On the command of '3' pupils move to the allotted place.

This chapter has set out in detail what cooperative learning consists of and has provided guidance on some of the necessary conditions for it to flourish. The next chapter will set out the steps needed to implement cooperative learning effectively.

Professional development activities

This chapter has included the following CPD activities:

Activity 4.1: PIGS F. Graphic representation of key elements of cooperative learning.

Activity 4.2: Incorporating PIGS F in lessons. Reviewing steps.

Activity 4.3: Planning lessons with partner work.

Points to remember

1. To be truly cooperative, group work should include five key elements known by the acronym PIGS F.

2. Cooperative learning consists of different types: informal cooperative learning involving partner work can be planned into any lesson. Formal cooperative learning requires teams to be set up and specific teamwork skills.

3. Cooperative learning works for two main reasons: improving motivation and through peers supporting each other towards the next step in their learning.

4. Cooperative learning can support higher-order thinking skills by carefully structuring partner and group work.

5. The teacher's role changes to be 'a guide on the side' creating the conditions for learning.

6. The formation of groups requires careful consideration and providing roles within groups can help structure the interaction and learning.

7. Classroom management for cooperative learning requires specific techniques which support a positive ethos.

Further reading

Aronson, E., Blaney, N., Sikes, J., Stephan, C. and Snapp, M. (1978) *The jigsaw classroom.* Beverly Hills, CA: Sage.

Brown, D. and Thomson, C. (2000) *Cooperative Learning in New Zealand Schools.* Palmerston: Dunmore Press.

Cohen, E. (1986/1994) *Designing Groupwork: Strategies for the Heterogeneous Classroom.* New York: Teachers College Press.

Johnson, D.W. and Johnson, R.T. (1999) *Learning Together and Alone: Cooperation, Competitive and Individualistic Learning.* Boston, MA: Allyn & Bacon.

Kagan, S. (1994) *Cooperative Learning.* San Juan Capistrano, CA: Kagan Cooperative Learning.

Sharan, S. (1990) *Cooperative Learning: Theory and Research.* Westport, CT: Praeger.

Slavin, R.E. (1995) *Cooperative Learning: Theory, Research, and Practice.* Boston, MA: Allyn & Bacon.

CHAPTER 5

A Step-by-Step Approach

This chapter provides detailed guidance on the steps necessary to effectively implement cooperative learning. This includes developing the right ethos and cohesion, team-building, resolving conflict and teaching the necessary skills.

Developing cooperative learning in steps

Before a group can successfully work together, it is vitally important to allocate time to team-building activities. Whilst it may seem that in a busy and overcrowded curriculum there is no time for such activities, research has shown that this is time well spent.

A summary of the steps in implementing cooperative learning can be found in Appendix 6. You will also find more discussion on this in Chapter 7.

Step 1: Class cohesion

The first step towards creating good teams is to create class cohesion. Here it is important for the teacher to get to know the pupils and their needs. A detrimental effect for the whole class can ensue if some pupils are socially isolated or having particular difficulties. One way of obtaining an overview of the pupils and their feelings towards each other is to ask them to note who they get along with and who they do not know well, and then to analyse these for particular problems. This can be done by giving each child a list of all the names in the class. Ask them to circle the names in green of those that are their special friends. They circle in orange those they would like to know and then circle in red those they do not know at all.

For younger pupils you could print small digital photos of children in the class and ask them to complete the same exercise, perhaps working with a small group at a time to complete this.

Pupils' choices	Pupils in class by number											
	1	2	3	4	5	6	7	8	9	10	11	12 etc.
Pupil 1												
Pupil 2												
Etc.												

Figure 5.1   Pupils' choices

Codes: L = like the most

O = know least well

B = like to know better

Analysing the data

Using a grid as shown in Figure 5.1, or similar using a spreadsheet on the computer, enter the codes for each pupil by the corresponding pupil(s) in the class.

Analysis of this information can help support mechanisms and create possible classroom buddies. Once having established an overview of the children in the class, it will form an important start to any school year to ensure that children get to know each other and 'learn how to be a friend'. Look at the suggested activities below and select suitable ones for use in your school and/or class.

Getting to know you activities

The following are a range of possible activities to ensure that pupils have the chance to get to know each other:

Human treasure hunt

Pupils are given a question sheet (see Figure 5.2 for an example) to fill in themselves and then they must find someone else who shares the same answer. He or she must sign his or her name next to the corresponding question. They have to circulate around the class until the sheet is completed. This can be formally structured by using a 1-2-3 move and having pupils move in a clockwise direction around the tables in the classroom.

Circle time

Sessions can take a similar format as the human treasure hunt by having sentence starters such as 'My favourite television programme is … '. Additional circle time activities that support getting to know each other are:

- **Name games** – students sit in a circle and say their name in turn. The aim of the game is to see how quickly they can get around the circle. Repeat and time. Go round the other way with everyone saying the name of the person on their right, then the person on their left.

- **Sharing similarities** – teacher asks the pupils to find someone who shares something, for example wearing the same colour socks, same number of brothers and sisters, and so on, and then swap places.

- **Just like me** – students sit in a circle and the teacher, or a pupil, says 'I went to the beach in the holidays', everyone who did the same says 'Just like me' and stands up. A variation is to have everyone with something the same, for example who likes tuna sandwiches, to stand up and change places. If there is one chair short (it starts with someone standing) then there is always someone left who has to say something.

	Myself	A friend
1. Favourite colour		
2. Favourite TV Programme		
3. Favourite food		
4. Dream holiday		
5. Favourite sport		
6. At weekends I like to ...		

Figure 5.2   Human treasure hurt

Photocopiable: Cooperative Learning in the Classroom
Paul Chapman Publishing © 2007 Wendy Jolliffe

Other class-building activities

- **Form a horseshoe** – in order of the initial of their first names. Once everyone is lined up, they can say who they are and one thing about themselves, for example favourite hobby, food, television programme, and so on. The teacher can note similarities and differences and model valuing diversity.

- **Line ups** – line up according to some dimension, for example height, number of pets owned, distance to school, and so on. It can work well to time this to see if they can beat their own 'record'.

- **Make a class logo, banner, song, rap, cheer, and so on** – create a distinctive sign by asking children to identify, first, individually three ways they would like the class to be special, then to share with a partner and then to share with another pair. Groups can then report to the whole class in a variety of ways, such as putting their three top things on a sticky note which is added to the class list. The class can then sort them into types and vote on the top three or more. Using this information, children can create a graphical representation.

Learning how to be a friend

Some of the following activities can form useful additions to a PSHE programme:

Friendly/unfriendly top 10

Divide the class into pairs. Ask each pair to brainstorm ways to be friendly and unfriendly. Ask each pair to share their list with another pair to become a group of four. Ask the group to agree on one in particular for each category. Then the groups report back to the class one friendly and one unfriendly behaviour, which the teacher writes on a flip chart or board. The class vote on a top five or 10 for each and the lists are printed later for display in the classroom.

A class book about friends

In this activity, children are asked to work in pairs to write examples of what being a good friend is. The teacher could begin by completing one in shared writing and then the children work together to write other examples. These are then collected into a class book and can be illustrated.

Parables

Published stories are effective ways of helping children to see the value of friendship and how to avoid the problems that fictional characters may have. There are a range of useful texts suggested in the SEAL resources. Parables that contain a message or fables that contain a moral can also be useful. The following are two further suggestions. The goose story is often used in Canadian schools to encourage children to think about the value of cooperating. Here is a variation of it for use with older children.

Goose Story

In autumn when you see geese heading south for the winter, flying in a V formation, think about why they do this.

As each bird flaps its wings, it creates uplift for the bird immediately following. By flying in a V formation, the whole flock adds at least 71 per cent flying range more than if each bird flew on its own.

When a goose falls out of formation, it suddenly feels the drag and resistance of trying to go it alone and quickly gets back into formation to take advantage of the lifting power of the bird in front.

When the head goose gets tired, it rotates back in the wing and another goose flies at the point.

Geese honk from behind to encourage those up front to keep up their speed.

When a goose gets sick or is wounded by gunshot and falls out of formation, two other geese fall out with that goose and follow it down to lend help and protection. They stay with that fallen goose until it is able to fly or until it dies, and only then do they launch out on their own or with another formation to catch up with their group.

If we have the sense of a goose, we will stand by each other like that.

Follow up questions:

- Do people who share the same purpose get on better?
- Does it help to take turns with difficult jobs?
- How can we encourage others?
- How does it feel to know that you will get help if you are in difficulty?

Class meetings

Having spent time getting to know each other and developing friendships, it is important for classes to have a regular time to reflect on progress and solve problems. Class meetings fulfil the following functions:

- announcements
- mutual support
- problem-solving
- improving
- planning events
- celebrating.

Proponents of cooperative learning have found that regular class meetings can be a powerful tool for teaching mutual respect, caring and cooperative attitudes. Guidelines for holding class meetings are:

1. Meetings need to be regular (preferably weekly).
2. There should be an agenda and only items on it can be discussed. Items for the agenda can be placed in a box in the classroom.
3. Pupils can take turns to chair the meeting after the teacher has modelled the process.

Activity

Review the above methods of developing class cohesion with colleagues and select those that are appropriate.

Step 2: Team-building

Once a sense of class cohesion has been built up, usually at the beginning of the school year and revisited from time to time, particularly at the beginning of a new term, it is important to work on developing team-building skills. This is a vital stage to ensure success, and should not be omitted. Five purposes have been identified for team-building:[1] (1) getting acquainted, (2) team identity, (3) mutual support, (4) valuing differences, and (5) developing synergy. Team-building also develops in sequential stages. It is useful to think of these as small steps within the whole process of developing cooperative learning.

Stage	Activities	Comments
A. Getting to know each other	*All in a circle* *Exchanging passports* *Biographical details*	
B. Beginning working together	*Rotating leaders* *The checker* *Tokens for talking* *Monitoring talk* *Numbered heads* *Triads*	
C. Working together	*Learning partners* *Random partners* *Fours* *Taking roles* *Solving problems*	
D. Reflecting and reviewing	*Top 10* *Reflective writing* *Observations*	

Figure 5.3   Stages in Team-Building

Now, with a colleague, examine the stages in team-building (summarised in Figure 5.3) and highlight the supporting activities that have a particular appeal for the children in your class with comments.

A. Getting to know each other

This is an important part of feeling included and is vital for psychological well-being. Activities include the following.

All in a circle

This can be done by forming a doughnut – two concentric circles facing each other (see structures, Appendix 3). The teacher gives the following directions at short intervals with a person from the inner circle taking a turn first, then the outer circle:

- Introduce yourself.
- Say what you like to do at weekends.
- Say what you like best at school.

Now ask the children from the outer circle to move several places around the circle until they are facing someone else. Ask them to repeat the process. You can repeat this as time allows.

Exchanging passports

Each pupil is given a small booklet, which can be made by folding two A4 pages in half and stapling them together. The teacher then asks them to do the following, with younger children writing and drawing pictures:

- On the front cover write your full name.
- On the first page write your address.
- On the second page write the place where you were born.
- On the third page write the names of any brothers or sisters or pets.
- On the following pages add hobbies or things you like to do out of school, favourite films, books or television programmes.

Pupils make pairs, or are directed to a partner and exchange passports. Then pupils introduce their partner to the class or to a group.

Biographical details

Pupils are paired off to find out information about each other and then to write a biography about their partner. This forms a class booklet which the teacher can share or older children can read for themselves.

B. Beginning working together

This is the stage after getting to know each other, when children can either test the teacher's power or try and assert power over each other. The following can help establish a more cooperative classroom:

- *Rotating leaders* – here the pupils in the class are given a number (which could be the same as the number in the register). The teacher then selects four numbers each week (either at random and marked off on a list, or in order) and those four pupils are the class leaders for the week. The role of the leader is to help the teacher – give out resources, run errands, and so on. They also meet once a week (at a break or lunchtime) with the teacher to discuss things that are going well and not so well. This can then be fed back to a whole-class meeting.

- *What did I say?* Here pupils paraphrase what a partner has said. This will need modelling by the teacher and pairs of pupils.

- *Talking tokens (see Fig. 5.3)* – give tokens to everyone in the group and when they want to talk, they have to put a token in the middle of the table. They can speak only as long as their tokens last. (See Appendix 3.)

- *The checker* – one person in a group is given the role of checking to see if everyone gets the chance to speak.

- *Numbered heads* – see structures (Appendix 3).

- *Triads* – class in groups of three with roles: pupil, helper, observer. The pupil asks for help with learning something, the helper coaches and the observer reports what was/ was not helpful.

C. Working together

Once time has been spent getting to know each other and beginning to work together, pupils can begin to work more productively together. The use of roles (see Appendix 5) can support this process. These are task roles and maintenance roles. The task roles focus on the content of the work and the maintenance roles focus on the social–emotional needs of the group. Typical task roles are brainstorming ideas, giving information, asking appropriate questions, clarifying or elaborating, summarising the learning, testing and assessing. Maintenance roles are encouraging others to contribute, checking each other's feelings, reconciling differences, compromising, ensuring all have a chance to speak. There needs to be time set aside to reflect on these aspects. This time will not be wasted as it will support learning. The following can be used to support this phase, to help academic goals and build self-esteem:

1. *Learning partners* – for example, check and coach (see Appendix 3) or response partners with guidelines. The teacher should model such activities and provide support.

2. *Random partners* – a way of getting pupils into different pairs quickly is to number pupils and then ask odd numbers to pair with the next even number; with young children colours can be used.

3. *Fours* – here pairs can join with another pair to make a group of four. Each member takes one fourth of the task and is responsible for learning it and then teaching it to the others.

4. *Taking roles* – the teacher gives out role cards (see Appendix 5) to assign roles to groups. This can be developed further to specific maintenance roles or task roles. This can be modelled by one group having roles assigned and then performing a short task while the others observe.

5. *Solving problems* – this can be used for a range of problems or conflicts and needs a stepped approach: (a) state the problem, (b) analyse it (c) suggest solutions, (d) plans for action, (e) possible outcomes, and (f) evaluating. For more details see Step 3 on conflict resolution (page 65). Older children may like to work in pairs to answer 'Agony Aunt' type letters which you provide with typical problems found by working with others in school, for example 'My partner won't talk to me', etc.

D. Reflecting and reviewing

This relates to continuous development and improvement, and can be done by:

1. **Top 10** – here children are given a short time, often during a plenary session, to identify one or two particularly good features of work with partners or groups in a lesson. These could be written on a sticky note and then placed on a notice board to review at the end of the week and celebrate success, such as a 'Top 10'.

2. **Reflective writing** (for example in a learning log) which can be completing a series of sentences, for example:

   (a) This week I did well at helping my partner …
   (b) To help all of us learn more, my partner/ group/ should …
   (c) One thing I will work on next is …

Good listening	Good questioning	Good encouraging	Good praising	Good supporting

Figure 5.4 **Observing good cooperative work**

Photocopiable: Cooperative Learning in the Classroom
Paul Chapman Publishing © 2007 Wendy Jolliffe

3. **Using pupils to carry out observations** – here it is important to stress positive behaviour, and pupils may like to highlight groups or pairs rather than individuals. Providing some prompts can be helpful (see Figure 5.4).

Step 3: Being able to resolve conflict

Conflict is a part of everyday life. My sister and I recently had the following conversation:

'Are my children normal?' she asked.
'Why do you ask?' I replied, looking at two lovely healthy children, 7 and 9 years old.
'Well, they are always arguing,' she said.
'Oh, absolutely normal, 'I replied, 'it's just sibling rivalry.'

Conflict is inevitable in any group. It is important to help children realise this and that it can be positive. It is important for teachers also to understand the dynamics. Too often teachers feel that any conflict is bad and avoid it at all costs. It is important to recognise its inevitability and to develop strategies to handle conflict.

Let us first look more closely at what conflict involves. Conflict varies. It can be:

- **Procedural** – about a course of action. This is the easier type to resolve and in the classroom can be solved by having clear agreed rules and regular class meetings and discussions.

- **Goal conflict** – about values or ends, such as pupils arguing over who will sit in a certain special chair. This can be more complex but needs discussion to agree on common goals.

- **Conceptual conflict** – over ideas, theories or opinions. This can be a good source of learning as pupils are required to state and refine their views, and can be well used for discussion purposes.

- **Interpersonal** – different personal styles. This is the most difficult type to handle but can best be dealt with by allowing differing pupils a voice and then 'agreeing to disagree'. A third party or mediator may be needed.

Procedures for conflict resolution

These should be taught to all ages of pupils. The underlying principles behind successful conflict resolution are, first, being able to stop and calm down and, secondly, being able to see another person's point of view. Many pupils do not know how to deal with disagreements. They may engage in personal attacks or 'put downs', get up and walk away, or even become physically abusive. Unless strategies are developed to deal with conflict, cooperative group work will not be successful. Research[2] shows how conflict escalates with the cycle of blaming, so that when a pupil is put down ('he told me my ideas stink', 'she told me to shut up', and so on) they can refuse to work together. Using 'I feel' statements is a good way to defuse the situation. Here the pupil translates

I feel statements

Share with the class the following examples of common conflicts in the classroom which consist of 'you' statements and then contrast them with 'I feel' statements.

Scenario 1: A member of the group interrupts you constantly when you are talking.

'You' statement: 'You're so rude! You never let me say anything!'

'I feel' statement: 'I feel really hurt when you interrupt me because I think what I have to say is important too.'

Scenario 2: One person in the group is messing around and not doing any work.

'You' statement: 'You're just lazy! You never do any work!'

'I feel' statement: 'I feel let down because you don't do any work and we need everyone to help to finish this activity.'

Scenario 3: One person in the group laughs at someone's ideas.

'You' statement: 'You're just stupid, that's why you are laughing.'

'I feel' statement: 'I feel hurt when you laugh because it feels like my ideas are not worth anything.'

Now provide the following negative 'You' statements and ask pupils to work together to come up with positive 'I feel' statements:

1.   Stop interrupting me!

2.   Stop messing around!

3.   Don't be rude!

4.   Don't keep all the pens for yourself!

5.   Stop talking and let others have a say!

Figure 5.5   I feel statements

What's the real message?

1. Two pupils in a group of four sit next to each other and hold the information sheet so the others cannot see it.

2. During a group discussion about homework, every time one pupil speaks the others show by facial expression that the person's ideas are not accepted.

3. As one person joins the group, another member shows he/she does not want this person.

4. Every time one person speaks in a group, the others look bored and not interested.

Figure 5.6   What is the real message?

the blaming statements into 'I feel' statements in which they express honestly how they feel in response to the other's statement or behaviour. For example, a pupil might say, 'I feel like no one wants to listen to me or work with me when you say my ideas stink.' This provides an opportunity for the other person to explain the basis for the negative statement and the situation is defused.

Look now at Figure 5.5 which consists of three scenarios which could be used for role-play activities in the classroom. Discuss these with colleagues and develop the use of 'I feel' statements. Adapt as necessary, developing your own scenarios and using them with the children.

It is also important to bear in mind that it is not only what people say to each other that causes problems, but also the body language that signals rejection. You may like to follow the activities in Chapter 3 for non-verbal communication and to spend some time looking at the negative effects of body language in the context of conflict resolution. Body language includes facial expression, posture and gestures. This can be demonstrated well with role play. A series of situations (see the suggestions in Figure 5.6) can be given to groups in the class and then, as they each act them out with a minimum of talking, the rest of the class has to decide on the message the body language is giving.

One successful way of supporting conflict resolution is to teach, model and practise using a peace path (Figure 5.7), as developed by Robert Slavin.[3]

Pupils can be trained to act as playground monitors/supporters to provide cooling-off times and to support others by use of the peace path. In addition, special places can be designated in schools, with books, posters and games about human feelings, which can support the overall process. These could contain writing materials for thank you notes, apologies or drawings. It

---

The Peace Path

Step 1: Take turns to state your feelings using an 'I' message:

   I feel .... when you ....

   I would like you to ....

Step 2: Suggest a solution

Step 3: Restate the other's solution

Step 4: Agree a solution

Step 5: Depart in peace

Figure 5.7   Peace path

could also act as a place for referrals for problems, for exemplary behaviour, a meeting place for ongoing problem-solving and for anger management. For any discipline problems a sheet containing the following is completed by the child before an adult confers with that child:

1.   Write, draw or tell what happened.

2.   Write, draw or tell your you feel about it.

3.   Write, draw or tell how you might have done differently.

4.   What should happen next?

These can also be used within classrooms.

Step 4: Teaching the skills

Developing cooperative learning in the classroom requires the prerequisites of class and team cohesion, and the teacher's ability to plan suitable activities and use appropriate structures, but it is also dependent on pupils having the small-group and interpersonal skills necessary to carry it out. In Chapters 2 and 3, developing interpersonal and communication skills as discussed as key factors. It is important to tease out more precisely what we mean by teamwork skills and then look at a step-by-step approach to teaching them.

Teamwork skills

It is useful first to distinguish task skills from working relationship skills. Task skills are focused on the content of the task and can be described as:

- generating and elaborating on ideas
- following instructions
- staying on task
- managing time successfully
- planning and reviewing progress.

Working relationship skills are focused on positive relationships in the group and can be described as:

- helping and encouraging each other
- everyone participating
- showing appreciation
- reaching agreement.

Working relationship or interpersonal skills can be more complex to teach. However, using what are called 'Skillsbuilder' exercises[4] can be helpful. The following activities support these skills.

Helping and encouraging each other

Key Stage 1. Groups of two or three children are each provided with assorted sticky-paper shapes and a larger piece of sugar paper. They need to help each other to create an animal or creature from the shapes, which has to suit the shape of the background paper. The group has to decide on a name for the creation. The teacher had to decide whether all shapes provided were used and whether the animal was recognisable.

Key Stage 2+: five-square puzzle. This activity is commonly used in cooperative learning.[5] Pupils in groups of five are given exactly enough pieces to construct five complete squares, but no individual can do it with just the pieces they have; only giving pieces to others is allowed, no taking and no talking. Each pupil has pieces marked only A, B, C, D or E. The group must end up with a complete square in front of everyone. This supports interdependence.

Resources: puzzles copied onto card and enlarged to about A5 size (see Figure 5.8), one puzzle per group of five (if the number of pupils in the class is not a multiple of five, make as many groups of five as possible, with spare pupils becoming observers to see how well pupils help each other).

Procedure:

- Pupils are in groups of five at tables.
- Each pupil has a set of pieces all marked with the same letter (A, B, C, D, or E).

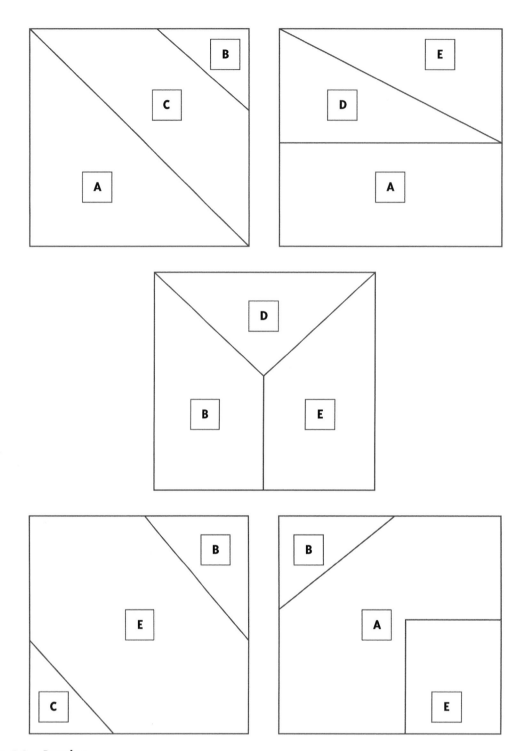

Figure 5.8   Puzzles

- Each pupil must make one square.

- No pupil may talk, signal or gesture to give help to others.

- Only giving is allowed, no taking.

- Except for any pieces given to others, pieces must be in front of each pupil.

- To complete the task all pupils must have completed squares in front of them.

After carrying out the activity it is important to spend time discussing which behaviours are helpful.

Everyone participating: jigsaws

Key Stage 1.

Resources: One page from a comic strip is cut into separate compartments and each piece is mounted onto backing paper so that the comic strip can be reassembled.

Procedure: the group is asked to place them in the correct order. For added difficulty one piece is missing and the group has to decide where the gap it.

Key Stage 2

Resources: one piece of written material is cut into separate sections for each group. Each section should be one or two complete sentences. A sheet of paper and some glue is needed for each group.

Procedure:

- Pupils need to be in groups of four.

- Each pupil takes one card and reads it to the group.

- After everyone has read their card they have to decide on the order and then stick the cards onto the paper.

- Roles such as timekeeper and participation checker can provide support.

- Groups have a set amount of time to complete the task.

Showing appreciation

Affirmation chips (can be used at any age). This is where pupils are given a certain number of tokens (such as counters) and are instructed to use them up during group work. They use one by saying something positive about another member of the team.

Cheerleader (most ages). Appointing a cheerleader in a group can support the team's appreciation of the input of different members. He or she can ask the group to pick their favourite positive adjectives, for example 'brilliant' or 'wicked', and at key points, when a team member has contributed something or as directed by the teacher, they chant their chosen word three times, for example 'wicked, wicked, wicked'. Teams can also choose 'cheers' to celebrate their team's success, such as 'a round of applause' where they clap silently in a large circular motion.

Reaching agreement

Dilemma situations. Here pupils work in groups of four and are given a dilemma to discuss (for example 'Best of friends', see Figure 5.9). Before the discussion the teacher should explain the skills that are necessary for the group to succeed (specifically reaching agreement) and roles are agreed in groups of timekeeper, participation checker and summariser.

Best of Friends

Susie and Max were what Susie's mum called 'attached at the hip'. They had been friends since they were small but, as they had become teenagers, it became more than that. They were boyfriend and girlfriend. One summer's evening, Max was walking Susie home. He had his new bike so he could ride back home. He was a keen biker and this was the latest model. As they walked along the path that led along the river, Max suddenly tripped and fell. He crashed headlong into the river still holding his bike. Susie let out a scream and rushed to help him. Max had landed on a rock at the side of the river. The handlebars of his bike were just visible. Susie managed to grab Max's hand and pull him out of the river, but his leg was badly smashed.

'You had better go and get help,' Max told Susie. She wrapped her coat round him and then ran as fast as she could to the main road. As she ran along towards the nearest house, a car pulled up. Susie looked round and saw James, an older boy from school who had just passed his driving test.

'Are you alright?' he asked.

Susie explained what had happened and asked for his help. James has always thought Susie was very pretty and agreed to help, but only if she gave him a kiss. Susie felt like telling him to get lost, but she needed his help and it was getting dark, so she climbed into the car and gave him a quick kiss. But James insisted that she agreed to be his partner at the school prom. She tried hard to persuade James that she couldn't but he was only going to help her if she went out with him. Finally she agreed.

Later after Susie managed with James's help to get Max home and the doctor had examined his injuries, she explained what she had to do to get help. To her amazement, Max was furious and said he never wanted to see her again. She was really upset as she had tried her best to help him and the next day she told James what had happened.

'Don't worry,' said James. 'I will get even with him for you.'

Some time later when Max was fully recovered and his bike had been repaired, he rode in through the school gates but, as he went to lock up his bike, he was set on by James. Susie watched smiling as James kicked Max so hard on his injured leg, he screamed in pain. To make it worse, the bike was stamped on and twisted out of shape once more.

Now discuss the roles of the characters in this story and rank them 'best' to 'worst': Susie, Max and James. Give reasons for your decisions.

Figure 5.9   Best of Friends

Levels of cooperative learning skills

The progression in developing cooperative learning skills has been described[6] as consisting of four levels:

1. Forming – the basic skills needed to establish the group.

2. Functioning – the skills needed for managing the group's activities to complete the task and maintain good relationships.

3. Formulating – the skills needed to build a deeper understanding of the material being studied.

4. Fermenting – thinking and cooperative skills needed to function at a high level.

In order to involve children in the progression of cooperative learning skills, it may be helpful to liken it to a four-stage rocket and gradually as each stage is added it becomes ready for blast off. To make this accessible to children, the wording of forming, functioning, formulating and fermenting has been changed. Figure 5.10 below shows this visually.

Professional development activity: reviewing potential problems

One of the issues that can hinder progression in cooperative learning is what to do when children are reluctant to work with peers, which can disrupt the smooth running of the group. Review the 'common social problems', in Appendix 9, with colleagues and discuss possible solutions. The next section which deals with teaching the necessary skills is also a crucial element.

Stages in teaching the skills

Each of the cooperative learning skills needs to be taught specifically in stages as follows (see the example Figure 3.2, page 33) for an example of this process related to active listening).

Establish the need for the skill

■ Brainstorm the skills needed – the best way to do this is to carry out a role play that demonstrates why the skill is needed (see Figure 5.11).

■ Discuss factors that helped.

■ Discuss factors that hindered.

■ Teacher poses 'What if … ' scenarios (for example, what if everyone left the group when they felt like it?).

Defining the skill

■ Use a T chart (see Figure 5.12). Draw a large T on the board or on a large piece of paper and either side of the T mark 'looks like', and 'sounds like' and with the class drawing up a list of what the skills sound like and look like. A double T chart can be used with older pupils to also include 'feels like'. This can then form a poster in the classroom for constant reference while the skill is practised and refined.

Guided practice

■ Provide opportunities for pupils to practise with corrective feedback. Encouraging feedback helps pupils persist and in the early stages feedback is needed more often.

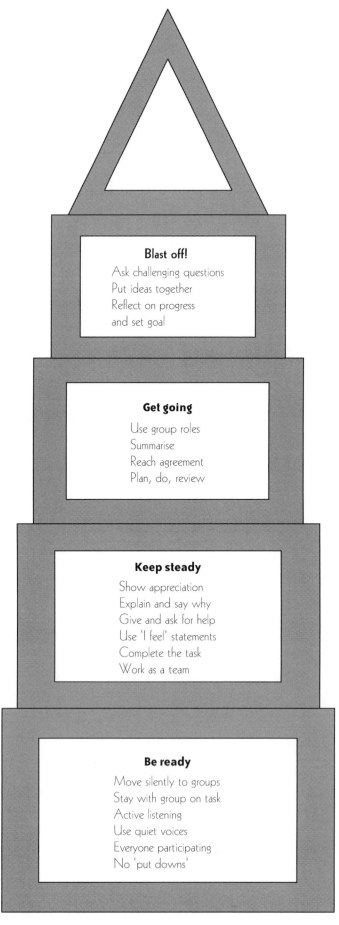

Blast off!
Ask challenging questions
Put ideas together
Reflect on progress
and set goal

Get going
Use group roles
Summarise
Reach agreement
Plan, do, review

Keep steady
Show appreciation
Explain and say why
Give and ask for help
Use 'I feel' statements
Complete the task
Work as a team

Be ready
Move silently to groups
Stay with group on task
Active listening
Use quiet voices
Everyone participating
No 'put downs'

Figure 5.10 The four-stage rocket of cooperative learning skills

Role play for 'everyone participating'

Choose four pupils and explain that you (the teacher) will take the role of another member in the group.

Play a game, e.g. five square puzzle where you need to make five squares and cannot talk or take pieces, you can only help and give pieces to others.

Role play not participating, e.g. by keeping your pieces and sulking.

After discussion, you may like to play the game again, this time with everyone participating, and discuss the difference.

Figure 5.11   Role play for 'everyone participating'

- The teacher monitors, observes, intervenes, coaches, reinforces and encourages. A major task is to observe the level of group skills, identify areas of need and provide coaching where necessary.

- Group reflection is an essential element in developing group skills. Groups reflect on how well they practised the skill and how they could become more effective in using it. This reflection should occur at some point during the lesson, rather than at the end and thus avoid it being left out.

Generalised application of the skill

- Once the skill has been established, the teacher provides opportunities for using the skill in a range of contexts. The group reflection sheet could include a section where pupils identify other situations where the skill could be used.

Professional development activity

Now look carefully at the cooperative learning skills needed for successful group work and at the four-stage rocket which demonstrates the progression in developing these skills. Working with colleagues, develop a plan for teaching and developing these skills in school. An action planning format is included as Appendix 7 to support this. See Chapter 7 for details on whole-school implementation and professional development activities.

Step 5: Incorporating cooperative learning into lessons

The next step is to incorporate cooperative learning into lessons. This is examined in detail in the next chapter; however, it is important to realise that this itself can be achieved in stages, as follows:

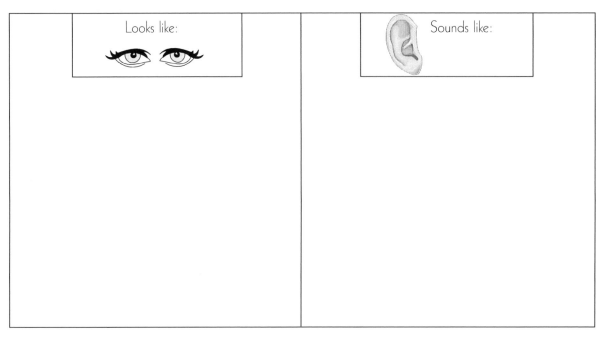

Figure 5.12   T chart

1. use paired work or informal cooperative learning, as discussed in Chapter 4, pp. 43–4.

2. Develop simple teamwork, by combining two pairs (twos to fours).

3. Begin coordinated teamwork by assigning management roles (such as materials manager, organiser, recorder and checker).

4. Teamwork requires individuals to each develop a separate part of the task and then this is shared.

5. More complex problem-solving teamwork with development of roles.

Professional development activities

This chapter has included the following CPD activities:

Activity 5.1: Developing class cohesion. Reviewing methods.

Getting to know you activities.

Activity 5.2: Reviewing stages in team-building and selecting activities.

Activity 5.3: Using 'I feel' statements and adapting them for use in the classroom.

Activity 5.4: The four-stage rocket – developing teamwork skills.

Activity 5.5: Possible issues – common social problems.

Activity 5.6: Developing an action plan for teaching and developing cooperative learning skills.

Points to remember

Implementing cooperative learning should be done in small steps consisting of five stages:

1. Class cohesion.

2. Team-building.

3. Resolving conflict.

4. Teaching the skills required in a progression of forming, functioning, formulating and fermenting.

5. Incorporating cooperative learning into lessons.

Further reading

Cohen, E. (1994) *Designing groupwork: Strategies for the heterogeneous classroom.* New York: Teachers College Press.

Johnson, D.W., Johnson, R.T. and Holubec, E.J. (1998) *Cooperation in the Classroom.* Edina, MN, Interaction Book Company.

Slavin, R.E. (1995) *Cooperative Learning: Theory, Research, and Practice.* Boston, MA: Allyn & Bacon.

Smuck, R.A. and Smuck, P.A. (2001) *Group Processes in the Classroom.* 8th edn. New York: McGraw-Hill.

CHAPTER 6

Putting Cooperative Learning into Practice

> This chapter looks at examples of putting cooperative learning into practice in lessons. It supports lesson planning and provides guidance on assessment with links to assessment for learning.

The previous chapter set out the steps to implementing cooperative learning ending with Step 5, that is, how to incorporate it into lessons. This will now be examined in detail.

Incorporating cooperative learning into lessons

The majority of lessons will benefit from informal cooperative learning, using learning partners as discussed on page 43. Figure 6.1 illustrates the benefits of providing partner work to support learning across the curriculum. See also Appendix 8 for a range of quick cooperative learning starter activities.

Which lessons are most suitable?

Formal cooperative learning where pupils are working together in small groups or teams must begin with team-building activities and pupils will need to have at least been explicitly taught the skills of cooperating at the forming or first stage of the four-stage rocket (see Figure 5.10). Once this is begun, the teacher can decide which lessons are most suitable for cooperative group work. Work with a colleague to examine the decision tree in Figure 6.2 to help you decide on a suitable lesson as a starting point.

Foundation Stage/Key Stage 1 Literacy

After reading the story *Handa's Surprise* by Eileen Browne, children were asked to think about the order in which the animals and fruit appear in the story. The children then discussed with a partner and came to an agreement about the correct order in which the animals and fruit appeared. Pairs then recorded their findings orally or in picture form. The teacher invited pairs to share their findings with the rest of the class.

Key Stage 1 Maths (Making own word problems)

The teacher presented a simple number sentence on the board and shared this with the group. The teacher then discussed with the children the numbers, symbols and operational vocabulary appropriate to the number sentence. The teacher then modelled the process of formulating a word problem from this number sentence. The children were given a similar number sentence on the board and a few minutes to think about a word problem that would match the new number sentence. The children were then given time to share their word problem to match the number sentence with their partner. Children shared their word problem with the rest of the group, who worked through the word problem on a whiteboard.

Key Stage 2 Geography (Tornados topic)

The class explored explanation texts presented on the interactive whiteboard. The children were then asked to think on an individual level about what they had just read and about any prior knowledge that they had gained in previous lessons and experiences. The children were then asked to share their knowledge with their partners. This information was then shared with the class and key points used to annotate the explanation on the interactive whiteboard.

Key Stage 3 Maths

In a Year 9 lesson on Mode, Median and Mean, students are working in learning partnerships which have already been established. The students work in A/B pairs to solve problems, and the teacher selects one student from each pair to answer. When questioned, the students express a preference for working with a partner, as they can explain the work to each other.

Figure 6.1 Examples of informal cooperative learning (with acknowledgement to facilitators from Bransholme Networked Learning Community)

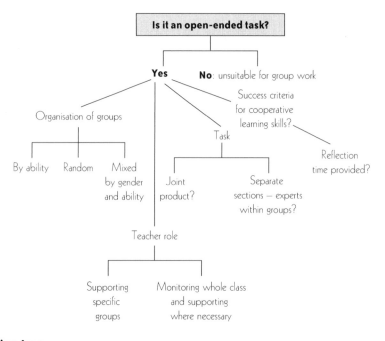

Figure 6.2 Decision tree

General issues for lesson planning

The following factors are key in ensuring effective learning when planning lessons incorporating cooperative learning:

1. **Activitate prior knowledge** (what do they know/understand already?). Provide opportunities for pupils to reflect on this, using structures such as think/pair/share, think/write/pair, and so on.

2. **Introduce the specific aspect of learning and where possible provide links to other current learning** (that is, present the 'big picture'). Explain the objective with success criteria and the necessary cooperative learning skills for the task. Choose one skill that you will focus on.

3. **Provide whole-class input interspersed with opportunities for paired talk**. Include modelling of tasks and so on.

4. **Guided practice**: here pupils work in pairs or groups to complete the task. The teacher must ensure that during this time he or she:

    (a) Monitors by checking, first, that pupils understand the task (if several do not, then stop the whole class and re-explain the task). Later, circulate a second time to check that pupils are on task. Finally, circulate a third time to provide clear time limits for task completion.

    (b) Provides time for pupils to complete the task and to reflect on the success related to the learning objective and to the particular skill identified.

5. **Plenary**: here pupils need to feed back on the task and how well they worked together. The teacher must decide the methods of feedback, which could include one or more of the following cooperative learning structures (see Appendix 3 for details):

    (a) Numbered Heads – this ensures interdependence because every member of the group must be able to answer for the group.

    (b) Two stay and two stray – two members of the group join another group to discuss how they completed the task and then return to their original group to feedback.

    (c) Doughnut – the whole class forms two circles with the inside circle facing outwards and the outside circle facing inwards. The inside circle talks about the task to the outside circle and then, on a signal, the outside circle moves several places. Now facing a new partner, the outside circle shares their own and their previous partner's thoughts on the task.

    (d) Whiteboard share – one member from each team posts an answer or particular points on the whiteboard.

    (e) Roam the room – groups place a summary, poster or completed task on their table and, on a signal, move around the room to the next table. In this way each group is able to view every group's products.

Other decisions that need to be made are:

1. Should informal (paired work) or formal work be included (or both)?

2. What cooperative learning skills are required?

3. How will groups be formed?

4. How many will be in each group?

5. How will the classroom be arranged (if you are planning group work then pupils need to be seated together facing each other)?

6. What time will be needed for the group task?

7. How will resources be organised?

8. Will each group have roles such as 'gofer' (resources manager), scribe, timekeeper, participation checker?

Selecting structures

Another important consideration is which structures should be selected. In order to become better acquainted with the range of structures, look at Appendix 3 and then select suitable structures to fit the scenarios in Figure 6.3 with colleagues.

Figure 6.4 may help in deciding when and where to use different structures.

Scenario	Possible structure(s)
Teams do not know each other well and have just formed.	
Pairs and groups need to listen carefully to one another and offer constructive feedback.	
Some pupils dominate group discussion.	
The teacher wants to ensure that every member of the group shares his/her ideas.	
The teacher is looking for new ways of feeding back to the class after group activities.	
The teacher wants to make sure that individuals have learned key aspects.	

Figure 6.3   Selecting structures

 Photocopiable: Cooperative Learning in the Classroom
Paul Chapman Publishing © 2007 Wendy Jolliffe

Planning a lesson

Now work with a colleague to plan a lesson that incorporates elements of cooperative learning. It is best to start small with paired work and gradually introduce group work as pupils gain the skills required. Try and spend time afterwards reflecting on what went well and what are the next steps. See also the section in Chapter 7 on peer coaching to support this.

Aspects of lesson	Cooperative learning structure
Introduction/activating prior knowledge Presenting the learning	Think/pair/share Think/write/compare Think/pair/square Round table Rally table Doughnut
Whole-class work/teacher input	Think/pair/share Think/pair/square
Guided practice/group work	Twos to fours Information sharing Jigsaw Grid Roving reporter Round robin Round table Graphic organisers Diamond ranking Talking tokens Check and coach
Plenary/reflection on learning and cooperative learning skills	Think/pair/share Think/pair/square Roam the room Doughnut Numbered heads Team interview Whiteboard share

Figure 6.4   Matching structures to parts of lessons

Examples of lesson plans incorporating cooperative learning

The following lesson plans are examples of cooperative learning in the Foundation Stage, Key Stage 1 and Key Stage 2. These lessons incorporate paired and group work and preliminary work on teaching the teamwork skills has been undertaken to a minimum of stage 2 (functioning level). Read these with a colleague and discuss:

■ How has cooperative learning supported the children to learn together?

■ How can you adapt these for work in your school?

Lesson 1: Foundation Stage: Communication, Language and Literacy

Learning objective: To listen carefully and retell the main points of a traditional tale.

Cooperative learning skills: To be an active listener, to take turns.

Resources: Copy of the story of *Little Red Hen*, props for the story (pictures of characters: Little Red Hen, cat, dog, pig, seeds, dried wheat or grass, flour, loaf of bread), sequencing pictures for the story.

Introduction:
Explain the objective and the cooperative learning skill.
Ask the children what they know about the story of the Little Red Hen and making bread using think/pair/share.

Whole-class work:
Read the story to the children using the props.
Ask the children why the Little Red Hen would not share the bread she made using think/pair/share.
Ask the children whether the cat, dog and pig in the story were good friends to the Little Red Hen using think/pair/share.
Now ask the children to tell their partner what the cat, dog and pig could have done to show they were good friends.
Now ask the children to work with another pair to share their ideas.
Ask for groups to share their ideas.

Focused group work:
Working with a small group of pupils using the props, help them to sequence the story. Ask children in pairs to put the pictures in the right order.
Pairs share the sequences.
Give out pictures to pairs of pupils and ask them to tell that part of the story.

Plenary:
Later in the day with the class together, retell the story of the Little Red Hen choosing children to take the parts and use the props.
Children listen carefully.
Ask children to review with partners how to be a good friend and help each other.
Finally, ask children to give you thumbs up, down or horizontal if they managed to listen well and take turns with their partners.

Figure 6.5   Lesson plan 1

Lesson 2: Key Stage 1: Geography (Year 2)

Learning objective: To be able to identify how children live in different parts of the world.

Cooperative learning skills: To share ideas.

Resources: Copies of pictures downloaded from Oxfam.org.uk/coolplanet/kidsweb/wake up/

Introduction:
Begin by explaining the objective and success criteria and the cooperative learning skills.
Now ask children to think about different countries around the world and first to share with a partner. if they have been to another country
Ask them to think about how it might be different if you live in a very hot country and then talk to a partner. Do the same for a very cold country.

Whole-class work:
Use the photographs you have downloaded to introduce the differences. Ask pupils in pairs to think/write/compare their thoughts on each photograph.
Make a class list of some of the key points.

Group work:
Ask children to sit with their partners and provide one picture between each pair. Ask children to write as many questions as they can, based on that picture.
On signal ask children to swap pictures with another pair to read the questions they have written and add some more if possible.
Now ask children to work as a team to look for clues to answer the questions in each of their pictures.

Plenary:
Display each picture on the interactive whiteboard and teams take turns to ask the rest of the class their questions. Teams share possible answers.
Ensure time is provided for the teams to reflect on how well they worked as a group and identify three stars and a wish (three things they did well and one thing they could improve).

Figure 6.6   Lesson plan 2

Lesson 3: Key Stage 2: History (Year 5/6)

Learning objective: To identify key aspects of life in Victorian times.

Cooperative learning skills: Helping and encouraging each other, everyone participating.

Resources: KWL grids, pictures of life in Victorian times on interactive whiteboard, information sheets on clothing, work, education, housing.

Introduction:
Introduce the objective and success criteria for the lesson and the cooperative learning skills and explain you will be adding points to group scores for groups showing helpful behaviour and where everyone is taking part.
Ask the children to line up according to their knowledge about life in Victorian times, with one end representing those who know something about it and the other end those who know very little. Now ask the children who know little to move to face those who know most (so one long line becomes two lines facing each other). Use this to form groups of four which consist of two who know least and two who know most.
Ask children to sit in groups of four (if there is an odd number, make groups of three or five) and using a graphic organiser such as a KWL grid (what I know, what I want to know and what I learned) they take turns to write what they know, and want to know.

Whole-class work:
With the whole class, explain that they are each going to become experts about a certain aspect of life in Victorian times. Using pictures you have downloaded or scanned, discuss what they portray about the Victorians. Use think/pair/share to promote partner work.

Group work:
With children in groups, give each member of the group an information sheet on clothing, work, education, and housing. On a signal ask each member of the group to re-form as expert groups on each (so all those with information on housing move to make one larger group).
Give children 10–15 minutes to work together to draw a diagram or to note some key words that represent the information.
On a signal, children move back to their original groups and have to take turns to teach their groups the main information about their particular aspect.
Now explain that they are all going to answer questions on life in Victorian times, and give out a question sheet containing one or two questions for each topic. All members of the group must be able to answer all aspects and the questions are taken individually.
Provide the answers and ask children to mark their partner's question sheet. Ask teams to add up their team scores and then take the teams' scores. Give additional points related to cooperative learning skills and celebrate teams' success.

Plenary:
Give teams a few minutes to rate themselves, on a scale from 1 (low) to 10 (high), on how well they did at helping and encouraging each other, and for everyone participating. Ask the team 'gofer' to display this on the class target board.

Now ask children to form a doughnut of an inner and outer circle and ask the inner circle to share what they can recall about life in Victorian times. On a signal, ask the children to move three paces clockwise and then ask the children on the outer circle to share what their previous partner said and add some things of their own.

Figure 6.7   Lesson plan 3

Review the lesson plans with colleagues and then plan and carry out a lesson incorporating some cooperative learning elements. Ensure you make time to review with a colleague, analysing what went well and what needs developing further.

Assessment of Cooperative group work

One of the issues and challenges for teachers when using cooperative learning is how to assess pupils' individual achievement, especially when there is such a strong emphasis on achieving targets in schools. However, two key points show that this potential problem can actually be a force for improved assessment and achievement. The first is the importance of involving pupils in the assessment – ensuring they understand the criteria and can assess themselves and peers against these. Cooperative learning lends itself to this process. The second is the need to balance group grades with individual assessment.

The following guidance can support the process:

Distinguishing assessment of cooperative learning skills from the assessment of learning

Whilst there is evidence that skills themselves contribute to the learning, for example the skills of help-seeking and help-giving impact on how much pupils learn from group work, generally process and product need to be separated. This will be supported by distinguishing the learning objective from the cooperative learning skill(s) being developed in lessons and evaluating them separately.

Use of peer evaluation

Studies have shown that sharing the responsibility for assessment between the teacher and pupils improves productivity and learning. Here the teaching of self- and peer-assessment procedures is helpful. The advantages of this are that it has been shown to provide pupils with a sense of ownership over their learning, it clarifies teacher expectations and helps to set targets for improvement. One key aspect is to provide pupils with clear criteria upon which to assess themselves and peers, which can be translated into grades or scores (often called rubrics). Studies have also found that involving pupils in assessment criteria so that they fully understand it, impacts positively on achievement.

Strategies to support self/peer evaluation

1. Use a learning log. These are typically exercise books in which pupils write their thoughts on aspects of their learning. Teachers may wish to structure them with headings such as 'What I did well' and 'What I need to work on', and so on. Pupils are regularly given a few minutes to write in their logs and then, if desired, give them to teachers to read. Teachers may comment, but not mark them. Many teachers have found this a useful tool in establishing relationships and trust between themselves and pupils, and a way of helping pupils to be more self-reflective.

2. Always provide time for reflection on learning and cooperative learning skills within the lesson. One simple strategy is to use three stars and a wish to help children identify three things they did well and one they feel they could improve on. A quick showing of 'thumbs up' (or down, or horizontal) can also display how well they feel they are doing at a particular aspect.

3. Provide training in self/peer assessment. Research[1] with children in the equivalent of Year 5 used a four-stage process consisting of:

    (a) Involve students in defining evaluation criteria,
    (b) Teach students how to apply the criteria,
    (c) Give students feedback on their self-evaluations,
    (d) Help students use evaluation data to develop action plans.

Important aspects here are to ensure that criteria are shared and in child-friendly language. There are also opportunities to see aspects modelled by the teacher and/or pupil. Providing illustrations can also be helpful, for example in what constitutes a particular mark or level (such as in an extract of writing).

Supporting assessment for learning has been identified by the DfES as crucial to effective learning and teaching. Review the key characteristics of assessment for learning produced by the DfES (Figure 6.8) and discuss with colleagues the links to cooperative learning.

Key characteristics of assessment for learning	Links to cooperative learning
AfL is embedded in a view of learning and teaching, of which it is an essential part.	
AfL involves sharing learning goals with learners.	
AfL aims to help learners to know and to recognise the standards for which they are aiming.	
AfL involves learners in peer and self-assessment.	
AfL provides feedback which leads to learners recognising their next steps and how to take them.	
AfL is underpinned by the confidence that every learner can improve.	
AfL involves both learner and teacher reviewing and reflecting on assessment data.	

Figure 6.8   Key characteristics of assessment for learning

Learning Spellings

The following procedures should be undertaken:

• Seat pupils in groups (preferably of four pupils).

• Give a spelling test to pupils individually (and ensure no copying etc.) based on particular words being learned.

• Mark the spellings together.

• Ask the pupils to add up the total group score (appoint a scorer on each team for this purpose).

• Take in and display the group scores.

• Now ensure pupils understand some strategies to learn spellings (such as finding mnemonics for the 'tricky' part of the word – e.g. 'O U lucky duck' for the ending of could).

• Ask pupils to help each other to learn the words they got wrong and share strategies. Remind them that they will be retested and it is the success of the group that counts.

• After a suitable amount of time to practise and help each other, retest with each pupil undertaking the test individually.

• Mark as before and then take in group scores.

• Be prepared to be amazed!

Figure 6.9   Learning spellings

The use of group scores

These are generally better used for assessment of cooperative learning skills and involving pupils in setting targets for improvement. This process can also support the interdependence of the group to jointly improve on scores. This procedure can also be used effectively when assessing a group product. The example in Figure 6.9 of using group scores to improve pupils' spelling (which can be adapted for other curriculum areas) has also been found to be very effective not only for motivation to improve, but also in actual achievement gains. However, a general 'health warning' needs to be borne in mind if the use of group scores is used widely as it can mask issues

Score	Bonus points
Below 50	1
51–55	2
56–60	3
61–65	4
66–70	5
71–75	6
76–80	7
81–85	8
86–90	9
91+	10

Figure 6.10   Bonus points indicator

with underachieving pupils. What has been found to be effective, however, is that pupils bene-fit from paired/group work prior to an individual assessment taking place. The key point is to balance group grades with individual assessment.

Giving scores or grades

At various times giving scores may be appropriate depending on the task. The following are some possible ways of combining this with group work.

1. Give an individual score plus bonus points based on all members reaching a particular criterion. Here a group activity (with a criterion based on the cooperative learning skills, such as 'helping and encouraging each other') precedes an individual test, which is marked, the scores added together (as in the spelling lesson in Figure 6.9) plus the bonus score to give a total team score (although individual progress is also identified). Teams can be then awarded certificates, and so on as a 'super team' although it must be borne in mind that these should be given to all teams reaching an agreed level and there is not just one winner.

2. A group activity followed by an individual test which is aggregated into a group score but this time with points added for the lowest individual score (this encourages all team members to support each other to improve scores). In this case the teacher would clearly indicate the bonus points as in Figure 6.10

3. Average team members' scores and then award status as in 1 above.

All this assessment information can be displayed on a 'Class improvement chart' which shows group scores. You may like to show 'Most improved team' also.

Professional development activity

Review the discussion on methods of assessment. You will need to decide on school policy in relation to the following questions:

1. Will you provide objectives for each lesson that relate to the learning and to the cooperative learning skill which is receiving attention?

2. Will you ensure that each lesson provides time for reflection on the learning and development of particular cooperative learning skills?

3. Will you involve pupils in self and/or peer assessment, and if so how will you support this process?

4. Will you provide time for partner/group discussion and support prior to individual assessment?

5. Will you, when appropriate, provide group scores and celebrate teams' success?

Why is cooperative learning not used more?

If cooperative learning has an extensive pedigree of research (as cited in Chapter 4) showing its benefits, it is interesting to question why it is not used more. Possible reasons for this are:

1. The skills of working together cooperatively are not explicitly taught. It is vital that children are taught these skills if they are to succeed (as discussed in this chapter).

2. Pupils need support with social and emotional skills and in particular emotional intelligence (as discussed in Chapter 2). In any classroom there will be children who display particular difficulties (see Appendix 9 for some common social problems and possible solutions).

3. Pupils do not have the necessary communication skills to work with others (see Chapter 3 for ways to support this).

4. Teachers are not able to plan and manage talk effectively in the classroom (see Chapter 3 for guidance).

5. Teachers do not understand the five key elements of cooperative learning and how to incorporate them into lessons (explored in depth in Chapter 4).

6. A staged approach to implementing cooperative learning is not adopted and being too ambitious too soon leads to a lack of success (Appendix 6: five key steps to implementing cooperative learning, also explored in Chapter 7).

7. Teachers lack support from colleagues: it requires cooperation amongst staff as well as amongst pupils. (The aim of this book is to work cooperatively with colleagues to implement and develop cooperative learning.)

8. There may be a lack of whole-school vision that sees cooperative learning as being at the very heart of improving learning and teaching (this underpins the philosophy behind this book).

Having a clear understanding of cooperative learning and the steps to support its effective implementation will ensure that the above issues do not impede its progress. Developing a whole school vision will ensure that cooperative learning is put into practice, and details of this are set out in the next chapter.

Professional development activities

This chapter has included the following CPD activities:

Activity 6.1: Which lessons are most suitable? Using a decision tree.

Activity 6.2: Matching cooperative learning structures to scenarios.

Activity 6.3: Reviewing examples of lesson plans.

Activity 6.4: Assessment for learning: links to cooperative learning.

Activity 6.5: Key decisions on assessing group work.

Points to remember

1. The majority of lessons will benefit from informal cooperative learning using learning partners.

2. Formal cooperative learning in small groups or teams requires the pupils to have developed the skills of working cooperatively.

3. Open-ended activities lend themselves to cooperative group work.

4. Cooperative learning structures need to be selected to support different aspects of the learning.

5. Assessment of group work should ensure individual and group assessment, and that pupils are thoroughly involved in the process.

6. It is not more widely used because teachers and pupils need the necessary skills to make it work.

Further reading

Brown, D. and Thomson, C. (2000) *Cooperative Learning in New Zealand Schools.* Palmerston: Dunmore Press.

Johnson, D.W. and Johnson, R.T. (1999) *Learning Together and Alone: Cooperation, Competitive and Individualistic Learning.* Boston, MA: Allyn & Bacon.

Kagan, S. (1994) *Cooperative Learning.* San Juan Capistrano, CA: Kagan Cooperative Learning.

Developing a Whole-School Vision

This chapter shows how all the factors that impact on the successful implementation of cooperative learning fit together to ensure that it can be put into practice effectively. These factors include developing cooperative learning across different age ranges, putting together a whole-school professional development programme, creating an action plan, exploring coaching as an effective method of support, and methods of monitoring and review.

Creating a vision: working together cooperatively

Previous chapters have looked closely at how cooperative learning can not only provide an effective vehicle for learning, but also at how it can provide key life skills of communicating and working with others. Being convinced of the overwhelming evidence of its success forms the kernel of a vision: a vision for a powerful learning community. As one Chinese proverb says:

If you want one year of prosperity, grow grain.
If you want ten years of prosperity, grow trees.
If you want one hundred years of prosperity, grow people.

This chapter will show how this 'kernel' can become a whole-school ethos. This requires commitment and strong leadership from headteachers and senior managers to ensure that cooperation filters across every aspect of school life.

Creating a learning community

If staff and pupils work together cooperatively, a school becomes 'a learning community'.[1] Others have concluded that a theme that runs through successful schools is that pupils, teachers and parents all share a sense of community and shared purpose. A community enhances the sense of belonging and, in turn, this enhances the desire to learn.

So, what are the factors that help to create this learning community, a community that is committed to working together cooperatively? The following are fundamental to success:

1. A clear commitment to implementing cooperative learning, supported by understanding from all staff of what it involves.

2. Support and training. This should include a well-organised programme of training sessions, with opportunities for practice and support from peers, ideally in a peer coaching situation.

3. Concrete strategies and resources to support teachers in the classroom.

4. Implications for the whole curriculum considered and links made. This is particularly important for PSHE which will form the natural vehicle for teaching the small-group and interpersonal skills necessary.

5. A step-by-step programme for implementation, monitored and reviewed, and adjustments made where necessary.

6. The appointment of a member of staff as coordinator or facilitator to lead the implementation, with time provided to make this effective.

7. A willingness to change. This is a very different way of working and it requires risk-taking, that is, teachers need to try a range of strategies and evaluate the successes and inevitable problems they discover. Here the use of teams or peers to provide support will offer the most effective form of professional development.

8. A cycle of meetings with peers/teams that feed into whole-staff meetings, sharing progress. This can then form the bedrock of wider dissemination of work with parents and the community as well as neighbouring schools. For those schools already part of a networked learning community, this will also provide valuable support.

Implementation across the primary age range

Studies have shown that cooperative learning can work equally well with 5-year-olds or 50-year-olds. Its complexity will vary, but it is fascinating to watch a simple structure such as think/pair/share work with Foundation Stage children and equally well with university undergraduates. Why? Because we all benefit from being given time to think and then to talk to a peer before answering. The focus of this book is for primary pupils; however, the author has also worked in a similar fashion with students in higher education. Nevertheless, there are some important points to consider in developing cooperative learning across the age range. This revolves around two main considerations. First, build up slowly beginning by developing partner work. Obviously more complex team activities are too advanced for very young children. Second, begin early to teach the skills of working together cooperatively. Figure 7.1 is a time line to support what can be done and when, although it provides general guidance only and many cooperative learning structures are applicable across age groups. Resourceful teachers will adapt this according to the children they are working with.

Foundation Statge	Cooperative learning structures/activities	Resources/references
Emphasis will be on: ➤ Beginning teaching and practising interpersonal skills of active listening, making clear statements, helping and supporting each other (sharing, asking for help, being a friend) ➤ Developing partner work	Name games Just like me Circle time activities Cooperative play Learning how to be a friend Stories and rhymes Turn to your partner Think/pair/share	Chapter 3 Strategies for talk and communication skills Chapter 5 Getting to know you Class-building activities Appendix 3

Years 1/2	Cooperative learning structures/activities	Resources/references
Emphasis will be on: ➤ Developing and practising interpersonal skills of verbal and non-verbal communication, active listening, describing behaviours, helping and supporting each other ➤ Partner work ➤ Combining pairs Think/pair/share ➤ Different methods of sharing	Sharing similarities Active listening Examples of helping and encouraging each other Mix-freeze-pair Turn to your partner Twos to Fours Doughnut	Chapter 3 Strategies for talk and communication skills Chapter 5 Getting to know you activities Chapter 3 Stages in teaching active listening Chapter 5 Teamwork skills Appendix 3

Years 3/4	Cooperative learning structures/activities	Resources/references
Emphasis will be on: ➤ Teaching and practising interpersonal skills of effective communication using quiet voices, no 'put downs', everyone participating, explain and say why, use 'I feel' statements ➤ Simple teamwork	Non-verbal communication Making clear statements Human treasure hunt Conflict resolution Three-step interview Talking tokens Parables Think-pair-square Think-write-pair-compare Round robin Numbered heads together Two stay and two stray Timed talking	Chapter 3 Strategies for talk and communication skills Chapter 5 'What's the real message?' 'I feel' statements Appendix 3

Years 5/6	Cooperative learning structures/activities	Resources/references
Emphasis will be on: ➤ Teaching and practising interpersonal skills of clear communication, verbal and non-verbal, show appreciation and support, reach agreement, reflect and set goals ➤ Range of teamwork	Describing behaviours Checking impressions Conflict resolution Dilemma situations Five-square puzzle Group identity Jigsaw activities Line-ups Check and coach Rally table Graphic organisers	Chapter 3 Strategies for talk and communication skills Peace path Chapter 5 Teamwork skills Appendix 3 Chapter 6 See history lesson example

Figure 7.1   Implementing Cooperative Learning across the Primary Age Range

Professional development activity

Review the progression in Figure 7.1 and decide with colleagues how you will implement cooperative learning with different ages.

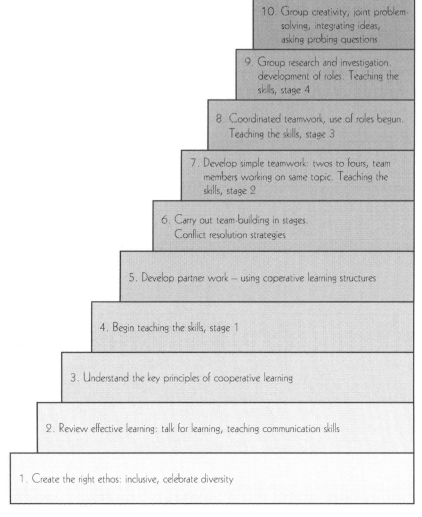

10. Group creativity, joint problem-solving, integrating ideas, asking probing questions

9. Group research and investigation, development of roles. Teaching the skills, stage 4

8. Coordinated teamwork, use of roles begun. Teaching the skills, stage 3

7. Develop simple teamwork: twos to fours, team members working on same topic. Teaching the skills, stage 2

6. Carry out team-building in stages. Conflict resolution strategies

5. Develop partner work – using coperative learning structures

4. Begin teaching the skills, stage 1

3. Understand the key principles of cooperative learning

2. Review effective learning: talk for learning, teaching communication skills

1. Create the right ethos: inclusive, celebrate diversity

Figure 7.2   A step-by-step approach to implementing cooperative learning

A step-by-step approach to whole-school implementation

Ten steps will ensure effective implementation (Figure 7.2). Each step will take some time to implement and it is particularly important to ensure that the first four steps are well established. Teachers will need to revisit stages and ensure each step in the process is secure, with opportunities for practice.

Professional development programme and calendar

The programme in Figure 7.3 is an approximate guide to allocating staff meetings and/or training days to implementing cooperative learning. The key aspects to bear in mind are that this will be achieved successfully through a mix of whole-staff discussion and training, and paired/team work to support implementation. The scheduling of weekly team meetings and setting up of paired coaching will also significantly impact on success (see page 102 for further details).

Term/session	Theme	Professional development activities	Whole staff/team/ individual	Approx. time required
Autumn	Inclusive practice	Read and discuss two scenarios Auditing inclusive practice	Individual and pairs preliminary reading	30 mins Over 1–2 weeks
Autumn staff meeting 1	Celebrating Diversity: Every Child Matters	Analysing audit Scenario 3: discuss ways to support Domains of emotional intelligence –adding strategies Strategies to support emotional intelligence	Whole-staff meeting	1 hour
Autumn staff meeting 2	Effective talk for learning	The ingredients for effective learning Stages in teaching active listening Managing talk in the classroom	Whole-staff meeting	1–1½ hours
Autumn staff meeting 3	Key elements of cooperative learning	Graphic representation of the five key elements Incorporating PIGS F in lessons: reviewing steps	Whole-staff meeting	1 hour
Autumn	Developing partner work	Planning lessons with partner work	In pairs	30 mins
Autumn	Reviewing partner work	Reviewing lessons taught	In teams	30 mins
Autumn	Creating conditions for cooperative learning	Developing class cohesion: reviewing methods	In pairs/teams	20 mins
Autumn staff meeting 4	Team-building Conflict resolution	Reviewing stages in team-building and selecting activities Using 'I feel' statements and adapting for use in the classroom	Whole-staff meeting	1 hour
Autumn staff meeting 5	Steps in teamwork skills	The four-stage rocket – developing teamwork skills	Whole-staff meeting	20 mins
Autumn	Reviewing teamwork Possible issues	Reviewing teaching teamwork skills Common social problems – reviewing solutions.	In teams	30 mins
Spring staff meeting 6	Developing a programme for implementation	Developing an action plan for teaching and developing cooperative learning skills	Whole-staff meeting	30 mins
Spring	Selecting appropriate lessons	Which lessons are most suitable? Using a decision tree Reviewing examples of lesson plans	In teams	20 mins
Spring staff meeting 7	Exploring the range of structures	Matching cooperative learning structures to scenarios	Whole-staff meeting	30 mins
Spring	Reviewing lessons taught	Reflection on lessons taught Possible issues and solutions	In teams	30 mins
Spring staff meeting 8	Assessment	Assessment for learning: links to cooperative learning Key decisions for assessing group work	Whole-staff meeting	1 hour
Spring	Review	Reviewing lessons taught Links to assessment for learning	In teams	30 mins
Summer staff meeting 9	Progression across the primary age range	Reviewing suggested progression and deciding on the most suitable	whole-staff meeting	30 min
Summer	Monitoring and assessment	Selecting appropriate monitoring strategies.	In teams	30 mins
Summer	Intervention	Strategies for intervention in group work	In teams/pairs	15 mins
Summer staff meeting 10	Review steps in implementation	Reviewing progress Revisit action plan and steps in implementation	Whole-staff meeting	1 hour

Figure 7.3   Professional development programme

Cooperative learning sample action plan

Area for development	Staff involved	Resource implications	Timescale	Review date
Staff training — key principles of cooperative learning	All staff	Whole-staff meeting	Sept 06	July 07
Developing class cohesion and team-building activities	All staff	Whole-staff meeting	Sept 06–July 07	July 06
Developing partner work	All staff	Team meetings	Oct 06–Dec 06	Jan 07
Skills teaching incorporated in PSHE	All staff	Team meetings	Oct 06–July 07	July 07
Developing a range of cooperative learning structures	All staff	Whole-staff meeting	Oct 06	July 07
Ensure co-operative learning has a high profile by modelling using facilitator. Observation data from teachers and peer coaching to identify strengths and areas for development	All staff	Timetable implications	Sept 06–Jan 07	April 07
Developing simple teamwork — peer coaching and facilitator support	All staff	Timetable implications	Mar 07–July 07	July 07
Reviewing skills teaching steps	All staff	Whole-staff meeting	Jan 07	July 07
Developing a range of cooperative learning structures	All staff	Whole-staff meeting	Jan 07	July 07
Develop teamwork, group research and problem-solving in the more able/older groups.	Years 5 and 6 staff, Facilitator	Meetings for Years 5/6 staff	April 07–Dec 07	Dec 07
Observation data from teachers and peer coaching to identify strengths and areas for development	All staff	Timetable implications Team meetings	June 07	Sept 07
Reviewing PSHE and skills development	SMT, PSHE Manager Facilitator	Timetable implications	June 06–July 07	July 07
Reviewing resources and sharing expertise	All staff, Facilitator	Team meetings	September 06–July 07	July 07

Figure 7.4   Sample action plan

Photocopiable: Cooperative Learning in the Classroom
Paul Chapman Publishing 2007 © Wendy Jolliffe

Action plan

One of the key jobs of the facilitator/coordinator is to ensure that the implementation matches the needs of the school. He or she will therefore need to complete an action plan that incorporates the steps in implementation (as in Figure 7.4) and the four-stage rocket of developing cooperative learning skills (Figure 5.10). A sample completed action plan is given in Figure 7.4. and a suggested format is provided as Appendix 7.

Learning with colleagues

One of the keys to implementing change in schools and to supporting effective professional development is to ensure that teachers work together cooperatively. The use of peer coaching (now called co-coaching) is increasingly being advocated by the DfES and government strategies as an effective way forward. Indeed, a National Framework for Mentoring and Coaching[2] has been established. This model involves teachers supporting each other in professional dialogue and ultimately improving practice. The key principles of cooperative work (positive interdependence, individual accountability, group processing/reflection, small-group and interpersonal skills and face-to-face interaction) apply equally to coaching and professional teams. The following are prerequisites for co-coaching in pairs, or for working in support teams:

- agreement on confidentiality

- agreement on a non-judgemental approach

- developing a basis for trust.

The purpose of this teamwork is to:

- help each other gain competence in using cooperative learning

- be an informal group to share, let off steam and discuss problems connected with implementing cooperative learning

- provide friendship and support.

The key activities of this support are:

1. Timetabled meetings to share successes and problems.

2. Opportunities to design, plan, prepare and evaluate lessons together that incorporate cooperative learning.

3. Organised times for team-teaching or reciprocal observations.

Reciprocal observations

Where possible, observing each other using cooperative learning in lessons will be beneficial both to the observer and the person being observed. It is important to be aware of the sensitivities of teachers when being observed. Keeping a positive stance is vital, as is realising that the job of the coach is not to note everything that could be improved but rather to focus on specific aspects agreed beforehand. The person coaching/observing should remember to remain non-judgemental and just comment on actual events and so on. The key point to realise is that this is a reciprocal arrangement and peers are helping and supporting each other. The following guidelines can ensure that these sessions are productive:

1. Discuss prior to the observation what particular area will be focused on. This may include particular pupils or any aspect of cooperative learning.

2. During the observation use a pro forma which shows the focus (see Appendix 10).

3. After the observation, ensure a discussion takes place as soon as possible. Ensure that feedback relates to what has taken place and not on general personal competence. Help each other to provide concrete and practical guidance on next steps. Above all, show recognition for the strengths in each other. It is too easy to be critical!

Team meetings

In addition to small-group or peer coaching, it is important for teachers to work in teams to support cooperative learning. This will typically be in age groups (such as Years 5/6) and the meetings may take place alongside other regular meetings. However, on a regular basis (preferably weekly), teams will need to discuss progress. If a coordinator (or facilitator) has been appointed, he or she should be present at all team meetings. The following is a typical agenda:

1. Start by reviewing cooperative learning elements and/or structures. This would work well using a structure such as rally table – passing a piece of paper to and fro in pairs and jotting a key word down each time, then comparing with another pair. You may also like to start by trying out a new cooperative learning structure.

2. Review lessons taught using cooperative learning, particularly what went well and any problems.

3. Discuss problems at some length to generate a number of possible solutions, so that each team member can select different things to try.

4. If there is time, jointly plan a lesson to teach the following week.

5. Decide on items for the next meeting.

School leadership

For cooperative learning to succeed, it is crucial for the headteacher and other senior managers in a school to ensure the following:

1. Create and maintain the vision: being really committed to developing a cooperative school that supports learning and essential social skills.

2. Appoint a facilitator/coordinator: having a member of staff responsible for the implementation and development of cooperative learning is a key factor in success.

3. Provide time: first, for the facilitator to carry out the task of monitoring and supporting staff and secondly for members of staff to be released from teaching to work with others in a team-teaching or peer-coaching situation.

4. Incorporate an in-school improvement plan: ensure identified steps in implementation included as a priority for school improvement. The cooperative learning action plan will inform these priorities.

5. Maintain focus: review progress regularly in staff meetings and ensure that time is provided for the phased professional development programme. Ensure success is celebrated.

Monitoring and review

Once cooperative groups start working, it is important to monitor progress. Monitoring starts with involving pupils in the process, then the teacher; and periodically the facilitator/ coordinator, in addition to other senior members of staff.

Pupils can be trained to be observers and will enjoy the responsibility this involves. The aim is to record and describe team members' behaviour and give pupils feedback. Pupils can be roving observers who circulate around the classroom to monitor all learning, or they can observe their own group by taking the role of observer. The following are some important points for guidance when observing:

1. Observers should not comment or intervene during group work until towards the end of the lesson (usually in a plenary) when groups review how well they have worked together.

2. Observers in teams should rotate so that each member has a turn.

3. The teacher and a pupil observer need an observation schedule to ensure that a specific focus is maintained.

4. Observation can be done by sampling at intervals (for example, every five minutes) pupils on task or fulfilling a certain agreed criterion (such as everyone participating) and recording the frequency.

5. The teacher might decide to focus on one particular group for the entire lesson and then rotate this during the week. He or she might also choose to observe each group for a few minutes at a time and proceed round every group during a lesson.

6. Observations can be structured in a variety of ways (using a pro forma) or be unstructured– making informal notes of pupils' actions, and so on.

7. It is very important to remember that observations are descriptive not interpretative. Observations record what happens and do not comment, for example, on how well pupils are working together. The skills of Foundation Stage practitioners here can be very fruitfully shared.

8. To make structured observations you need to decide on the following:

(a) Decide which skills you are focusing on (generally this will be the focus for the lesson and shared clearly with the pupils).

(b) Decide on the format of the observation proforma and how this is to be carried out, for example, frequency of recording actions.

(c) Decide on whether to observe all groups, or focus on one or two.

(d) Decide on when and how to give feedback to the pupils (this may be at the end of the lesson, or if you want more time to reflect on data, at the beginning of the next lesson).

(e) Decide on how groups will use the information and set targets for improvement.

Observation forms

Two examples of observation forms are given in Figures 7.5 and 7.6. Teachers will need to adapt these to fit the pupils/particular focus, and so on.

Professional development activity

Review and decide on appropriate methods for monitoring progress with colleagues/whole-school staff.

For Figure 7.5 observers put a tally mark against each pupil for every example of a specific behaviour seen and total these at the end of the lesson.

The checklist in Figure 7.6 can be used with the whole class when monitoring generally, or with specific groups.

Other observers

Proponents of cooperative learning suggest that visitors to the classroom should be put to good use! Rather than allow them to sit and watch, ask them to carefully observe the pupils and take on the role of roving observers with an observation form such as the checklist in Figure 7.6. Another suggestion[3] is to have a mystery person as the focus of observation: see Figure 7.7.

Intervening in cooperative group work

As you monitor and observe groups, sometimes it will be necessary to intervene. The key to knowing when is careful observation, which can help you ascertain what pupils understand and what skills they display. As pupils work together they make their thinking explicit to their teams members/partners. It is helpful to distinguish intervening to provide help with the task and intervening to provide help with interpersonal and small-group skills. One general point is to try and turn a problem back to the group so they find their own solution, rather than to impose one. The rule is try not to intervene unless really necessary. Figure 7.8 lists some ideas for intervening. It is essential to celebrate where key aspects are in place. Now discuss intervening in group work with a colleague.

	Pupil 1:	Pupil 2:	Pupil 3:	Pupil 4:
Positive interdependence (helping and encouraging each other)				
Individual accountability (everyone participating)				
Other				
Total				
Group total:				

Group: Observer:

Focus: Date:

Figure 7.5   Structured Observation Form

P **Photocopiable: Cooperative Learning in the Classroom**
Paul Chapman Publishing 2007 © Wendy Jolliffe

Behaviour	Yes	No	Comments
1. Do pupils understand the task?			
2. Are pupils supporting and helping each other?			
3. Is everyone participating?			
4. Are pupils working towards the success criteria?			

Figure 7.6   Checklist

P **Photocopiable: Cooperative Learning in the Classroom**
Paul Chapman Publishing 2007 © Wendy Jolliffe

Mystery Person

1. Tell the class you (or a visitor) will be focusing on one pupil whose name will be kept secret.

2. Observe during the lesson without showing who is being observed.

3. Describe what the person did (frequency, and so on) to the class during the plenary without naming the person.

4. Ask pupils to guess the mystery person's identity.

Figure 7.7   Mystery person

Look for:	If absent, suggest:
Team members sitting closely together	Put your chairs closer together.
Resources ready for the task	Have you got a 'gofer' to get everything ready?
Pupils have started the task	Let me see you get started. Do you know what to do?
Pupils are on task	Do you need any help?
A specific cooperative learning skill is being used.	Who can help John?
Reluctant pupils involved	I'm going to ask … to explain this. Help … and I'll come back soon.
Team members explaining to each other what they are learning and how	I'm going to ask each of you to explain this to me.
Groups working effectively	What is wrong here? Can we come up with different ways to solve the problem?
Groups have completed the task	You are being very thorough, but time is nearly up. Can you try and finish by …

Figure 7.8   Ideas for Intervening

Group name:					Class:
Date	On task work	Explaining ideas	Helping and supporting each other	Everyone participating	Completing tasks

Figure 7.9   Group Progress

 Photocopiable: Cooperative Learning in the Classroom
Paul Chapman Publishing © 2007 Wendy Jolliffe

Involving pupils

One effective way of measuring success in implementing cooperative learning is to ask the pupils. Appendix 11 contains a sample questionnaire to be given to pupils following a lesson that contains group work. This is designed for older children (Years 5/6), but could be adapted for younger ones or be read to them. After completion, use the following guide to help analyse the answers:

1. What percentage of the class found the task interesting?

2. What percentage of the class found the task too difficult or confusing?

3. How many pupils reported they did not interact/talk?

4. How many pupils stated they got along with half or fewer members of their group?

5. How many pupils reported that they had helped each other?

Analysing group effectiveness

One way to support reflection on group effectiveness amongst pupils and to support setting targets for improvement is to give them a weekly progress report. Figure 7.9 is an example.

Conclusion

This chapter has put together all the crucial aspects of implementing cooperative learning from leadership to training and practice. Having a clear step-by-step programme for teaching the skills of working cooperatively, and the introduction of a range of structures and activities, will provide the means to put cooperative learning into practice. It is important to bear in mind that this is not a 'quick fix' to issues such as behaviour and/or poor academic standards. It can certainly impact on both, but only if it is properly implemented, and this takes time following the steps provided here. It also requires a fundamental shift in the role of the teacher, as with cooperative learning the teacher facilitates the learning rather than being the imparter of knowledge. This shift, once made, releases the teacher to motivate, provide opportunities for learning, monitor and celebrate. To return to the anecdote, in the Introduction, of the Rip Van Winkle effect: the teacher has become a teacher of the twenty-first century.

In reaching this, however, there doubtless will be pitfalls along the way. Development will be tricky at times and persistence will be needed. This can be significantly aided by the appointment of a key member of staff to oversee and support cooperative learning, and by the use of peer coaching or small teams. Teachers may feel this is a high price to pay, but the benefits far outweigh the difficulties, The benefits are:

- pupils being motivated and really enjoying their learning

- academic success being supported by working with peers

- pupils' showing improved emotional intelligence.

In addition, benefits for staff in working together cooperatively will improve staff morale. In effect, cooperative learning has enormous potential for creating a real learning community: a community where every child really matters. Is this a community you want to join?

Professional development activities

This chapter has included the following activities:

Activity 7.1: Reviewing progression across the primary age range.

Activity 7.2: Methods of monitoring and review.

Activity 7.3: Strategies for intervening in group work.

Points to remember

1. By creating a vision for working together cooperatively, the school becomes a real learning community.

2. Cooperative learning can take place from the Foundation Stage and across the primary age range by selecting suitable methods and activities.

3. There are 10 main steps to effective implementation.

4. A clear timetable for professional development will ensure implementation is effective.

5. Facilitators/coordinators need to develop an action plan to support implementation.

6. Working cooperatively with colleagues in teams or in coaching pairs will significantly impact on success.

7. Methods of monitoring and reviewing progress should be determined.

8. Knowing how and when to intervene in groups is vital.

9. Involving pupils in reviewing progress can be very effective in the development of cooperative learning.

Further reading

GTC leaflet, at www.gtce.org.uk/pdfs/peer.pdf

Johnson, D.W., Johnson R.T. and Holubec, E.J. (1994) *Cooperative Learning in the Classroom.* Alexandria, VA: ASCD.

Johnson, D.W. and Johnson, R.T. (1999) *Learning Together and Alone: Cooperation, Competitive and Individualistic Learning.* Boston, MA: Allyn & Bacon.

Peer coaching: NUT programme: *The a-z of peer coaching,* at www.teachers.org.uk/cpd.

APPENDICES

Appendix 1   Cooperative Learning Professional Development Programme

Theme	Chapter/ PDA ref.	Professional development activities (PDAs): Think about this	Whole staff/ team/individual	Approx. time required
Every child matters	Intro I.3	Mapping the aims and outcomes of *Every Child Matters* with the advantages of cooperative learning	Whole staff meeting	30 mins
Inclusive practice	Chap 1 1.1, 1.2	Read and discuss two scenarios Auditing inclusive practice	Individual and pairs preliminary reading	30 mins Over 1–2 weeks
Celebrating diversity: every child matters	Chap 2 2.1 2.2 2.3	Scenario 3: Discuss ways to support Domains of emotional intelligence Fig 2.1 Strategies to support emotional intelligence	Whole staff meeting	1 hour
Effective talk for learning	Chap 3 3.1 3.2 3.3	Aspects of learning Stages in teaching active listening Managing talk in the classroom	Whole staff meeting	1 – 1½ hours
Key elements of cooperative learning	Chap 4 4.1 4.2–4.4	Graphic representation of the five key elements Incorporating PIGS F in lessons: reviewing steps	Whole staff meeting	1 hour
Developing partner work	Chap 4 4.5	Planning lessons with partner work	In pairs	30 mins
Reviewing partner work		Reviewing lessons taught	In teams	30 mins
Creating conditions for cooperative learning	Chap 5 5.1	Developing class cohesion: reviewing methods	In pairs/teams	20 mins
Team-building Conflict resolution	Chap 5 5.3 5.4	Reviewing stages in team-building and selecting activities Using 'I feel' statements and adapting for use in the classroom	Whole staff meeting	1 hour

Theme	Chapter/ PDA ref.	Professional development activities (PDAs): Think about this	Whole staff/ team/individual	Approx. time required
Steps in teamwork skills	Chap 5 5.10	The four-stage rocket – developing teamwork skills	Whole staff meeting	20 mins
Reviewing teamwork Possible issues	Chap 5 5.5 Appendix 9	Reviewing teaching teamwork skills Common social problems – reviewing solutions.	In teams	30 mins
Developing a programme for implementation	Chap 5 Appendix 7	Developing an action plan for teaching and developing cooperative learning skills	Whole staff meeting	30 mins
Selecting appropriate lessons	Chap 6 6.1 6.2 6.3	Which lessons are most suitable? Using a decision tree. Reviewing examples of lesson plans	In teams	20 mins
Exploring the range of structures	Chap 6 6.4 Appendix 3	Matching cooperative learning structures to scenarios	Whole staff meeting	30 mins
Reviewing lessons taught		Reflection on lessons taught Possible issues and solutions	In teams	30 mins
Assessment	Chap 5 6.8 6.5	Assessment for learning: links to cooperative learning Key decisions for assessing group work	Whole staff meeting	1 hour
Review		Reviewing lessons taught Links to assessment for learning	In teams	30 mins
Progression across the primary age range	Chap 7 Fig 7.1 7.1	Reviewing suggested progression and deciding on suitable one	whole staff meeting	30 mins
Monitoring and assessment	Chap 7	Selecting appropriate monitoring strategies.	In teams	30 mins
Intervention	Chap 7 7.3	Strategies for intervention in group work	In teams/pairs	15 mins
Review steps in implementation	Chap 7 7.2	Reviewing progress Revisit action plan and steps in implementation	Whole staff meeting	1 hour

Photocopiable: Cooperative Learning in the Classroom
Paul Chapman Publishing © 2007 Wendy Jolliffe

Appendix 2   Fulfilling Pupils' Needs

Look at the following aspects related to Maslow's hierarchy of needs (see page 2). How well do you provide for each at school?	
Need	**School provision**
Water	
Food: healthy snacks/fruit	
Regulation of heat	
Support for upset or worried pupils	
Support for bullied pupils	
Support for lonely/unliked pupils	
Conflict resolution procedures	
Celebrating different types of achievement	
Procedures if pupils are stuck/unable to do work	
Goals for learning and improvement shared with pupils	
Varied creative outlets for pupils	

Appendix 3   Cooperative Learning Structures

Class-building	Team-building	Thinking skills	Communication skills	Information sharing	Mastery
Human treasure hunt List of up to 10 questions given to each pupil. They have to find someone to answer each question who then elaborates and signs their name.	**Two truths and a lie** Teams take it in turns to tell two truths and a lie. Teams have to guess the lie.	**Think-pair-share** Teacher asks a question and then provides 'think' time, pupils talk to a partner and then share their answers.	**Timed talking** Pairs are given roles of A and B. Partner A talks for 60 seconds, partner B talks for 45 seconds and then partner A continues/summarises.	**Round robin** The teacher asks an open-ended question. Each member of the team takes turns to share their answer, orally or in writing. Class discussion of answers.	**Doughnut** Pupils stand in two concentric circles, facing each other. They share information on a topic learned. At a given signal the outside team moves a number of paces clockwise and shares what they have heard.
Line-ups Class lines up according to given criteria with the most knowledgeable at one end and the least at the other. The line is split into two, to make two lines. Mixed ability groups of four can be then made.	**Three-step interview** (e.g. sell your house) Teams work in pairs to describe something such as their house. Their partner then has to sell it to the team.	**Think-pair-square** Pupils are first given think time, they then share with a partner. Lastly they share thoughts with the rest of their team.	**Paraphrase game** After listening to a partner or member of the team, pupils should summarise or paraphrase what they have said. Team members listen for accurate paraphrasing.	**Team interview** This is like a round robin, except each pupil has an allotted amount of time and other members ask the student questions.	**Rally table** Pupils work in pairs to take turns to share ideas back and forth. These are often written down and passed to and fro. Pairs then share their lists and form a composite team list.
Mix-freeze-pair Pupils circulate and when the teacher says 'freeze', they stop. work When s/he calls 'pair', they form pairs and interview each other on suggested themes, e.g. pets, holidays, pop groups.	**Round robin** Teams respond in turn to a question from the teacher, either orally or in writing. It is legitimate to pass.	**Think-write-pair-compare** Here pupils jot down their thoughts before sharing with a partner, which helps organise thoughts and ensures individual accountability.	**Twos to Fours** Pairs work together and then share their ideas with another pair.	**Two stay and two stray** After working on a topic, two members of the team move to an adjoining team to share ideas. Pairs then move back to their original teams to compare.	**Numbered heads together** Each member of the team is a number and then asked to on a topic or answer a question. Numbers are then called at random and every member of the team must be able to respond.

Class-building	Team-building	Thinking skills	Communication skills	Information sharing	Mastery
Name games Pupils sit in a circle and say their name in turn. The aim is to see how quickly they can get round the circle saying first their names and then the person on their right/left, etc.	**Group identity – team logo/banner/name/ poster** Creating a product that reflects all the members of the team.	**Graphic organisers** See communication skills, but also useful for organising thoughts.	**Talking tokens** Each person in each team is given a 'token' (such as their pen). If they want to talk they have to place their token in the centre of the table. They cannot talk again until everyone has put their token in the centre.	**Roam the room** At a signal, pupils move about the room (often in a clockwise direction) to look at and discuss what other teams have done. Particularly useful after use of graphic organisers.	**Flashcard game** Where a subject requires the memorisation of facts (such as multiplication tables), pupils work in pairs with flashcards, showing question on one side, and the answer on the other. Pairs take turns to hold up questions and test each other on correct answers.
Just like me Pupils in a circle and the teacher says something they have done, or like. Everyone who did the same, says 'Just like me!' and stands up.	**Team hamburger or pet** Each member describes their favourite food or pet. Using art materials the team constructs one that reflects the interests of all.	**The grid** Using a four-by-three grid for each pupil with rows labelled such as 'what I learned', 'something I did not understand', 'something I found interesting'. They fill in for themselves and find other pupils to write their thoughts.	**Graphic organisers** These are ways of organising information which are produced and discussed by the team. Examples include the T chart, Venn diagrams, fishbone, ideas trees.	**Whiteboard share** Following from team work, such as three-step interview, one representative from each team posts their best answer on the board or flip chart.	**Pairs check/check and coach** After working on a topic, teams (or the teacher) prepare a list of questions to check understanding. Pairs take it in turns to answer the questions with the other partner prompting and coaching.
Sharing similarities Pupils are asked by the teacher to find someone who shares the same birthday, has read the same book, likes the same actor, etc.	**One and all** A framework (e.g. Venn diagram) for discovering similarities and differences of team members.	**Diamond ranking** Teams are given a series of nine statement cards and then decide how to rank them in a diamond with the most important at the top.	**Class value lines** An issue is stated. Students decide to stand at a point on the line representing what they think. They pair up with the person next to them and state their position.	**Roving reporter** While pupils are working on projects, one representative from each team may for a certain amount of time, be a 'roving reporter' gathering information from other teams.	**Roundtable** This is like round robin. Pupils write answers to a question and pass the paper round the table for everyone to contribute.

Appendix 4   Developing Effective Communication Skills – a Phased Programme

Stage	Skill	Activity	Follow up
1. Getting the message across	Verbal and non-verbal communication	Non-verbal communication – e.g. the 'window dresser' Communicating verbally in different situations – e.g. in the playground, talking to a visitor, booking a ticket on the telephone, talking to a close friend, talking to a large audience	Develop 'types of talk' Monitor effectiveness in different situations Setting personal goals
2. Receiving the message	Active listening	Teaching the skill in stages: (i) Establishing the need (ii) Defining the skill (iii) Guided practice (iv) Applying the skill	Defining the key aspects of active listening Developing key phrases or icons Monitoring effectiveness Setting personal goals
3. Making it clear	Making clear statements	Using limited words or sentences to state information clearly, for example: provide pairs of pupils with complex sentences One person shortens and clarifies. The other paraphrases it accurately. For support this can be done in groups of four with one pair helping each other to shorten and clarify the sentence, the other pair helping each other to paraphrase	Summarising or constructing a poster of how to make clear statements Monitoring effectiveness Setting personal goals
4. It is not just what you say, it is how you say it	Describing behaviours	Providing pairs or groups of four with sentences to be said in different ways, e.g. 'That's a very nice dress' said enviously, enthusiastically, critically. One person, says the sentence the others have to say the motive behind the statement	Key points to remember: that tone of voice can provide empathy or antipathy, and that it is important to be able to state the behaviour without making a value judgement Monitoring effectiveness of work with others and groups Setting personal goals
5. What you say shows how you are feeling	Checking impressions	Providing cards with a range of feelings, e.g. embarrassed, pleased, annoyed, surprised, impressed. Pupils work in pairs, observed by another pair to have a conversation with an everyday dialogue (about meeting each other, the weather, how they are, etc). conveying a specific feeling	Noting facial expression and body language as conveying feelings as well as words Monitoring effectiveness of work with others and groups Setting personal goals

Photocopiable: Cooperative Learning in the Classroom
Paul Chapman Publishing © 2007 Wendy Jolliffe

Appendix 5　Roles in Groups

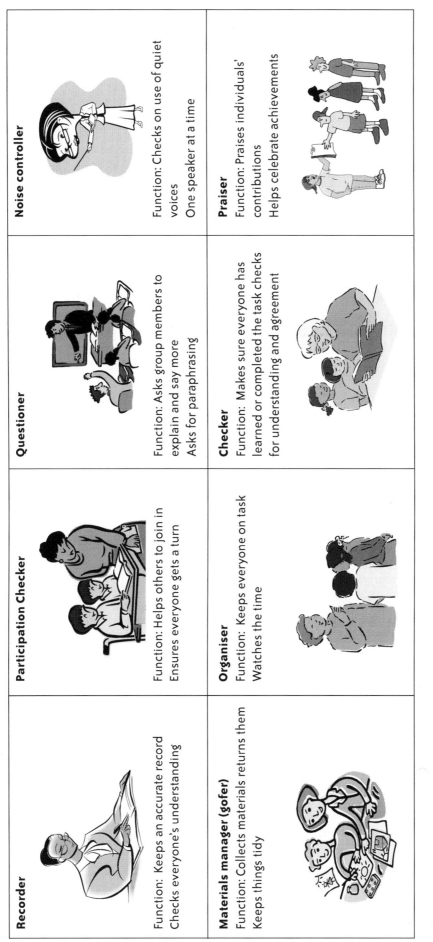

Recorder	Participation Checker	Noise controller
Function: Keeps an accurate record Checks everyone's understanding	Function: Helps others to join in Ensures everyone gets a turn	Function: Checks on use of quiet voices One speaker at a time
Materials manager (gofer)	Questioner	
Function: Collects materials returns them Keeps things tidy	Function: Asks group members to explain and say more Asks for paraphrasing	
	Organiser	Checker
	Function: Keeps everyone on task Watches the time	Function: Makes sure everyone has learned or completed the task checks for understanding and agreement
		Praiser
		Function: Praises individuals' contributions Helps celebrate achievements

Photocopiable: Cooperative Learning in the Classroom
Paul Chapman Publishing © 2007 Wendy Jolliffe

Appendix 6   Five Key Steps to Implement Cooperative Learning

Step	Title	Activities
Step 1	Class cohesion	Understanding class friendships Getting to know you activities Class-building activities Learning how to be a friend Class meetings
Step 2	Team-building	A. Getting to know each other B. Beginning to work together C. Working together D. Reflecting and reviewing
Step 3	Being able to resolve conflict	Procedures for conflict resolution Understanding body language Peace path
Step 4	Teaching the skills	Teamwork skills/skillsbuilder exercises Levels of cooperative learning skills (four-stage rocket) Stages in teaching the skills
Step 5	Incorporating cooperative learning into lessons	Partner work Choosing appropriate lessons Lesson planning Selecting cooperative learning structures Assessing cooperative group work

Appendix 7 Action Plan for Teaching and Developing Cooperative Learning Skills

Area for Development	Staff involved	Resource implications	Timescale	Review date
Staff training: key elements and team-building				
Allocate time/curriculum area(s)				
Incorporate in long-and medium-term plans				
Programme for teaching teamwork skills prepared				
Stage 1: Forming (Be ready)				
Stage 2: Functioning (Keep steady)				
Stage 3: Formulating (Get going)				
Stage 4: Fermenting (Blast off)				
Paired work incorporated				
Use of Cooperative learning structures in lessons				
Teamwork developing				

Stage 1: Forming (Move silently using 1-2-3 move, Stay with group on task, Active listening, Use quiet voices, Everyone participating, No 'put downs')
Stage 2: Functioning (Show appreciation and support, Explain and say why, Give and ask for help, Use 'I feel' statements, complete the task, work as team)
Stage 3: Formulating (Use group notes, Summarise, Reach agreement, Plan, do review)
Stage 4: Fermenting (Ask challenging questions, Put ideas together, Reflect on progress and set goals)

Photocopiable: Cooperative Learning in the Classroom
Paul Chapman Publishing © 2007 Wendy Jolliffe

Appendix 8   Quick Cooperative Learning Starter Activities

1. Turn to your partner: ask the pupils to turn to a partner and ask something about the lesson; explain a concept you have taught; explain the task; summarise an aspect of learning, or three important points, etc.

2. Reading triads: pupils work in threes to read a text and answer questions. One person is the reader, another is the recorder and the third the checker (who checks to make sure everyone understands and agrees the answers. When they have finished, they sign the answer sheet to show that they all understand and agree on the answers.

3. Jigsaw: pupils work in small groups and each person finds out about part of a topic then teaches what he/she has learned to the group.

4. Focus trios (or pairs):   before a new topic or lesson, pupils summarise what they already know about the topic and come up with questions/things they want to find out – this can be done on a graphic organiser such as a KWL grid (what I Know/want to know/what I have learned). They later discuss what they have learned and may add to a grid.

5. Drill partners: pupils drill each other on key facts until they are certain both partners know and can remember them (can be done with spelling, vocabulary, times tables, etc.). Individual tests can follow and bonus points be given for all members getting a certain score.

6. Reading buddies: pupils read to a partner, taking turns to read a sentence/paragraph/page each and the partner then summarises what has been read. This can also be applied to reading work to a partner, who then suggests something to add, improve, etc.

7. Worksheet checkmates: two pupils complete one worksheet with each having a different job, e.g. reader and writer, but both agree and support each other.

8. Homework checkers: pupils compare homework, discuss and agree a consensus. They staple the sheets together and receive one grade for the group. Alternatively they discuss and mark each other's work.

9. Writing pairs: pupils work together to produce a piece of writing. One can take the role of 'Creator' and the other the role of 'Writer'. They need to discuss ideas and agree before writing.

10. Computer groups: pupils work in trios: one to type, another to read material and the third to check that the task is completed. Roles are rotated.

Appendix 9 Cooperative Learning – Common Social Problems

Personality type	Possible solution	Comments
Mr Noisy	Role play of speaking loudly at inappropriate times. Demonstrate a 2 metre voice, 1 metre voice, half metre, 20 cm voice – children practise different voices. Assign a noise monitor to the group and/or class. Teacher monitors and praises those talking in quiet voices and makes it clear voice levels for different activities. Traffic light cards: green for good noise level, yellow for need to lower the volume, red for be quiet for 10 seconds and then resume quietly. Ask children to reflect on success of talking in quiet voices after group work.	
Miss Won't	If a child refuses to work with others, just let him or her withdraw temporarily. By observing the interaction of others over time, research has shown that most children will join in. Reinforce interdependence by assigning roles to groups and ensure that there are often fun warm-up activities. Have a focus for a week on everyone participating and reward groups for this. Give a lone child a role such as roving reporter to check on groups' progress. Structures such as roundtable and round robin can support participation.	
Mr Rejected	For a child that is unpopular and children are reluctant to work with consider carefully the make-up of groups and place the child with supportive pupils. Use group roles to encourage maximum participation. Use structures such as roundtable, round robin, three-step interview, pairs check.	

Personality type	Possible solution	Comments
Miss Shy	A shy pupil often finds it easier to talk to a partner rather than a group. Monitor for everyone participating and reward groups. Games such as 'broken squares' can support this where groups are each given pieces to make up four squares and they have help each other to build them without talking. In reflection time use round robin to say something they really like about another member of the team's contribution.	
Miss Bossy	When a pupil dominates ensure that groups are given different roles and one member checks that everyone contributes. Structures such as 'talking tokens' can help where everyone is given a number of counters, or tokens and to talk they have to place their counter in the middle of the table. They cannot talk again until everyone has placed their token in the centre.	
Mr Angry	If a child is hostile it may be necessary for him or her to have some 'time out' to cool off. A warning system of inappropriate behaviour using yellow and red cards can support also. Ensure that this is not a result of being rejected and that maximum participation is encouraged. Structures to help include affirmation tokens – where groups are given a number of counters to use up by saying something positive about a member of the group and putting into the centre of the table.	

Appendix 10   Cooperative Learning Peer Observation Pro Forma

N.B. Not all the questions for each part of the lesson may be applicable, and it may be preferable to comment solely on the area of focus.

Focus agreed: **Date:**

Part of lesson	Comments
Introduction/whole-class section ➢ Progress on area of focus? Other possible areas: ➢ Cooperative learning skill identified? ➢ Cooperative learning elements explained/modelled? ➢ Opportunities for paired work?	
Group work ➢ Progress on area of focus? Other possible areas: ➢ Pupils able to settle to the task quickly? ➢ Do pairs/teams show support for each other? ➢ Is everyone participating? ➢ Do the majority of pupils display the cooperative skill(s) required for the lesson? ➢ Teacher monitoring of groups? ➢ Use of cooperative learning structures? ➢ If a group has a problem, do the pupils know strategies without referring automatically to the teacher? ➢ Opportunities to acknowledge and celebrate success with cooperative learning skills?	
Plenary: ➢ Progress on area of focus? Other possible areas: ➢ Can pupils reflect on learning and cooperative learning skills? ➢ Methods of feedback? ➢ Everyone participating?	
Particular strengths:	

Appendix 11   Pupil Questionnaire

Please put a ring round the letter of answer that you think is most suitable for each question.

1. How interesting did you find your work in the group?

a) Very interesting   b) Fairly interesting

c) Quite interesting   d) Not interesting at all

2. How difficult did you find your work in the group?

a) Extremely difficult   b) Fairly difficult

c) Just about right   d) Very easy

3. Did you understand exactly what the group was supposed to do?

a) I knew exactly what to do b) At first I didn't understand

c) It was never clear

4. How many times approximately did you have the chance to talk during group work today?

a) None   b) Once or twice

c) Several times   d) A lot

5. If you talked less than you wanted to, what were the main reasons?

a) I felt afraid to give my   b) Somebody kept interrupting me
   opinion

c) I was not given the chance d) Nobody listened to me

6. Did you get on with everyone in your group?

a) With a few   b) With about half of them

c) With all of them   d) With none of them

7. Did you help each other with the task?

a) All the time   b) Most of the time

c) Sometimes   d) Not at all

8. Would you like to work with this group again?   a) Yes   b) No

Notes

Introduction

1. Alexander, R. (2004) Still no pedagogy? Principle, pragmatism and compliance in primary education, *Cambridge Journal of Education*, 34, 7–33.
2. Slavin, R.E. (1995) *Cooperative Learning: Theory, Research and Practice* 2nd edn. Boston, MA: Allyn & Bacon.
3. Galton, M., Hargreaves, L., Comber, C., Wall, D. and Pell, A. (1999) *Inside the Primary Classroom 20 Years On*. London: Routledge.
4. DfES (2004) *Excellence and Enjoyment: Learning and Teaching in the Primary Years*. Professional development materials (Ref: DfES 0519-2004), www.standards.dfes.gov.uk/
5. DfES (2005) *Excellence and Enjoyment: Social and Emotional Aspects of Learning*. (Ref: DfES 1319-2005), www.standards.dfes.gov.uk/
6. Johnson, D.W., Johnson, F.P. and Stanne, M. (2001) Cooperative learning methods: a meta-analysis, www.clcrc.com/pages/cl-methods.html

Chapter 1

1. Shachar, H. (2003) Who gains what from cooperative learning, an overview of eight studies, in R.M. Gillies and A.F. Ashman (eds), *Cooperative Learning, The Social and Intellectual Outcomes of Learning in Groups*. London: RoutledgeFalmer.
2. Slavin, R.E. (1996) *Education for All*, Lisse: Swets & Zeitlinger.
3. QCA (2000) *National Curriculum Handbook for Teachers*, Inclusion Statement, B. I. www.nc.uk.net/nc_resources/htm/inclusion.shtml (accessed 03.08.06)
4. Moyles, J., Hargreaves, L., Merry, R., Paterson, F. and Esarte-Sarries, V. (eds) (2003) *Interactive Teaching in the Primary School: Digging Deeper into Meanings*. Maidenhead: Open University Press.
5. Alexander, R. (2004) *Towards Dialogic Teaching*. Cambridge: Dialogos.
6. Brown D. and Thomson C. (2000) *Cooperative Learning in New Zealand Schools*. Palmerston North: Dunmore Press.
7. Johnson, D.W. and Johnson, R. (1985) The Internal dynamics of cooperative learning groups, in Slavin, R., Sharan, S., Kagan, S., Lazarowitz, R., Welbb, C. and Schmuck, R. (eds), *Learning to Cooperate, Cooperating to Learn*. New York: Plenum, (pp. 103–24).

Chapter 2

1. Gardner, H. (1983) *Frames of Mind: The Theory of Multiple Intelligences*. New York: Basic Books.
2. Claxton, G. (2002) *Building Learning Power*. Bristol: TLO Ltd, p. 98.
3. Goleman, D. (1995) *Emotional Intelligence*. New York: Bantam Books.
4. Csikszentmihalyi, M. (1990) *Flow: The Psychology of Optimal Experience*. San Francisco, CA: HarperPerennial.
5. DfES (2005) *Guidance on the 'Social and Emotional Aspects of Learning' (SEAL)*. (Ref: DfES 1319–2005.) London: DfES, p. 50.

6. DfES (2004) *Excellence amd Enjoyment: Social and Emotional Skills of Learning*. London: DfES, p. 7.

7. Johnson, D.W. and Johnson, R. (1999) *Learning Together and Alone: Cooperative, Competitive and Individualistic learning*, 5th edn. Needham Heights, MA: Allyn & Bacon.

Chapter 3

1. Corden, R. (2000) *Literacy and Learning through Talk: Strategies for the Primary Classroom*. Buckingham: Open University Press.

2. Edwards, 1992, cited in Mercer, N. (1995) *The Guided Construction of Knowledge: Talk amongst teachers and learners*. Clevedon: Multilingual Matters.

3. Vygotsky, L.S. (1978) *Mind in Society: the Development of Higher Psychological Processes*. Cambridge, MA: Harvard University Press.

4. Mercer, N. (2000) *Words and Minds: How We Use Language to Think Together*. London, Routledge, p. 11.

5. DfES/QCA (2003) *Speaking, Listening, Learning: Working with Children in Key Stages 1 and 2*. London: DfES/QCA.

6. Kelly, P. (2005) *Using Thinking Skills in the Primary Classroom*, London: Paul Chapman Publishing.

7. DfES/QCA (2003) *Speaking, Listening, Learning: Working with Children in Key Stages 1 and 2*. London: DfES/QCA. DfES (2005) *Speaking, Listening, Learning: working with children who have special educational needs*. London: DfES.

Chapter 4

1. Slavin, R.E. (1995) *Cooperative Learning: Theory, Research, and Practice*. Boston, MA: Allyn & Bacon.

2. Vygotsky, L.S. (1986) *Thought and Language*. Revd and ed by A. Kozulin. Cambridge, MA: MIT Press.

3. Sharan, S. (1990) *Cooperative Learning: Theory and Research*. Westport, CT: Praeger, Johnson, D.W., Johnson, F.P. and Stanne, M. (2001) Cooperative learning methods: a meta-analysis, www.clcrc.com/pages/cl-methods.html

4. Blatchford, P., Kutnick, P., Baines, E. and Galton, M. (2003) Towards a social pedagogy of classroom group work, *International Journal of Educational Research*, 39, 153–72.

5. Bloom, B.S. (1956) *Taxonomy of educational goals. Handbook 1: cognitive domain*. New York: McKay.

6. Johnson, D.W. and Johnson, R.T. (1999) *Learning Together and Alone: Cooperation, Competitive and Individualistic Learning*. Boston, MA: Allyn & Bacon.

Chapter 5

1. Kagan, S. (1994) *Cooperative Learning*. San Juan Capistrano, CA: Kagan Cooperative Learning.

2. Cohen, E. (1994) *Designing Groupwork: Strategies for the Heterogeneous classroom*. New York: Teachers College Press.

3. Slavin, R. (1996) *Education for All*. Lisse: Swets & Zeitlinger.

4. Cohen, E. (1994) *Designing Groupwork: Strategies for the Heterogeneous Classroom*. New York: Teachers College Press.

5. Smuck, R.A. and Smuck, P.A. (2001) *Group Processes in the Classroom*. 8th edn. New York: McGraw-Hill.

6. Johnson, D.W. and Johnson, R.T. (1999) *Learning Together and Alone: Cooperation, Competitive and Individualistic Learning*. Boston, MA: Allyn & Bacon.

Chapter 6

1. Ross, J.A., Rolheiser, C. and Hogaboam-Gray, A. (1999) Effects of self-evaluation training on narrative writing, *Assessing Writing*, 6(1), 107–32.

Chapter 7

1. CUREE/DfES, (2006) Mentoring and Coaching: CPD Capacity Building Project: National Framework for Mentoring and Coaching, www.curree.co.uk.
2. Johnson, D.W., Johnson R.T. and Holubec, E.J. (1994) *Cooperative Learning in the Classroom.* Alexandria, VA: ASCD.
3. Johnson, D.W. and Johnson, R.T. (1999) *Learning Together and Alone: Cooperation, Competitive and Individualistic Learning* Boston, MA: Allyn & Bacon.

*I*NDEX